The Niche Movement:

The New Rules to Finding the Career You Love

Kevin O'Connell

The Niche Movement: The New Rules to Finding the Career You Love

The Niche Movement

Washington, DC

www.thenichemovement.com

Copyright © 2015 Kevin P. O'Connell

Luke Owen Media (June 15, 2015)

ISBN: 1512078999
ISBN-13: 978-1512078992

*Without my mother and father's values and guidance,
this movement would not exist.*

*Thank you Mom and Dad for all that you do
and for shaping me into the man I am today.*

*Thank you to my amazing wife Courtney
for your love, support, and momentum
to make this book become a reality.*

CONTENTS

ACKNOWLEDGMENTS

The following individuals and Kickstarter supporters made this book possible.

Camille Sennett – A Niche Movement contributing editor and most importantly the brains behind our public relations and Kickstarter success in the summer of 2014. Thank you for all of your effort — your work ethic and drive will take you far.

Nicole Piquant – A young professional and recent graduate from American University I met in the fall of 2014 after moving to Washington, DC. Nicole was one of the first editors to touch this book and help compile all the interviews. Thank you.

Nicole Booz – Founder of GenTwenty, a Niche Movement contributor and an editor who came in at the fourth quarter to bring my stories to life and put the shine on this book.

Lilit Kalachyan – A fellow WeWork member and talented NYC based graphic designer responsible for the simplicity and design of the cover.

Robyn Fournier – The official editor of this book who went through it with a fine toothcomb. Thank you for all of your work.

And thank you to all of our Kickstarter supporters:

Jay Anandpara
Punit Arora
Katie Bean
Elizabeth Nicole Booz
Garry Bresett
Dave & Alice Bresett
Cortney Brewer
Michelle & Ben Brisson

Faina Bukher

Roger Calderon

Jennifer Caputo

Valerie Champagne

Laura Chegwidden-Jacobs

Christopher Conzen

Steph Cwynar

Kevin Dahaghi

Lucas Dalakian

Sabina De Matteo

Leah DeGraw

Ernie & Gail DeGraw

Joan DeGraw

Marylene Delbourg-Delphis

Christopher Dunlap

Nina Duong

Chris Earp

Kristin Eggers

Lori Enright

Melanie Feldman

Mike Fox

George Georgitsis

Michael Gerstein

John Giannone

Ellen D. Gnandt

Al Gordon

Mike Greenberg

Kristina Holme

Alex Hsu

Paul Kania

Charlie Kuski

Alison L.

Wout Laban

Joyce Lam

Michelle LaPlatney

Amma Marfo

Chris McAlpine

Maxwell Miller

Scott Montalbano

Remo Moomiaie-Qajar

William Moore

Amanda Morrison

Shannon & Jason O'Connell

Ronnie O'Neill

Kevin & Mary O'Connell

Michael P. Daley

Corrie Payson

Brittany Perkins

Kristen Pettis

Christine Presto

Erik Qualman

Kate Quinlan

Dustin Ramsdell

Nathan Resnick

Stacy Rinaldi-Campesi

Christian Ross

Shaunna Rubin

Brendan Scher

Sarah Shaw

Meredith Stille

Colleen & Don Stone

Kyle Stone

Courtney Stone O'Connell

Christopher Sutton

Bridget Thompson
Kwesi Vincent
Ben Wheelock
Benee Williams
Dana Wise
Megan Wyett
David Zygmunt
Grace Lee

Foreword

by Nancy Lyons

Human Resources departments around the globe are scrambling to imbed what they see as a hip new benefit called "work-life balance" into their programs — giving their employees the opportunity to prioritize between their careers and ambitions and their leisure and pleasure. As for me, founder of Clockwork, a Minneapolis-based tech company specializing in user experience, content, design, engagement and more, I believe Human Resources departments have it all wrong. I reject the idea that it is a work-life balance and instead simply refer to it as "life balance" because the reason for living is to do great work and have great lives.

Realistically, we bring our work home and we bring our lives to work.

It is this forward-thinking mindset on work culture that has landed me and my company, Clockwork, more than 16 Best Workplace awards. Some including Best Women Owned Business and Psychologically Healthy Workplace awards. Our team of 75 shares all successes because we have all worked really hard to achieve our goals together.

My road to success could be considered a long and bumpy one, but it has been worth the ride. I pursued a traditional path to a career in media but found myself in a man's world, making coffee runs for a boss whose dismissive, condescending actions served as catalysts for my future success as an entrepreneur. Despite his poor leadership style, my passion for technology never ceased — I could really see how technology has changed us and so my creative mind didn't care about the poor work atmosphere. Instead of sulking, I channeled that inner anger and frustration in the right direction and later opened Clockwork in a giant yellow building where my former boss drove by every day.

How's that?

As I reflected on my journey and realized that many of my partners had similar work histories — crappy bosses, crappy experiences — I've worked tirelessly since Clockwork's inception to develop a company with strong values that are actually demonstrated. It is not enough to simply state the company's values; they have to be lived. Understanding that we are creatures of habit and hype, I have revisited and published Clockwork's values regularly in order to create an ideal environment for our team.

Similarly, I have constructed a workspace that applauds purpose and teamwork. Whereas many companies focus on money and output, I believe that 150-year-old trend is dead and instead hope my employees feel connected to their work and not exploited like many other positions.

This story embodies what it means to find your niche. As a woman with big ideas and a graduate school dropout, I never let the pressures of traditional career moves or fears of failure hinder my job happiness. In fact, it's okay to fail! We live in a culture that prefers finished, polished and perfect — but in reality, we should go easy on ourselves because shame is pointless energy. Fall on your face and forgive yourself when you do, and then realize what you've learned as a result and give yourself credit for that.

Finding your niche involves exploring and, often, paying your dues on the way up, but that's okay. As you'll learn in this book, careers happen by accident. Becoming too hyper-focused on any one position could mean missing out on what was really meant for you.

- Nancy Lyons

Nancy speaks extensively about work culture, entrepreneurship, social media, technology and leadership and has been locally and nationally recognized for her role as owner and CEO of Clockwork.

Clockwork has received more than 16 "Best Workplace" awards. Clockwork has also won the Psychologically Healthy Workplace, Best Women Owned Business and Bicycle Friendly Business awards.

Independently, Nancy received the Minneapolis/St. Paul Business Journal Diversity in Business award and was a finalist for Minnesota Business Magazine's Community Impact award.

In June of 2014, Nancy spoke on the structure of the workplace at the inaugural White House Summit for Working Families in Washington, DC.

Introduction

"How do you know what you *do* want to do, if you haven't figured out what you *don't* want to do?"

A profound statement in itself, the line was coined by Nicole Piquant, a young, up-and-coming writer from New York City during our weekly meeting on a below 20-degree morning in January 2015 at our office in Washington, DC.

Without realizing it, Nicole, a recent graduate of American University, touched upon one of the visions for this book. In that moment, she recognized that she would not be where she was at 22 years old if it weren't for one simple action: trying new things. Less than seven months after graduation, Nicole is figuring it out in the so-called real world, but in an unconventional way. Most important to note, it is *her* way.

She doesn't follow anyone else's wishes, demands or even societal pressures. She experimented while in college, traveling abroad to Australia, holding various internships and enjoying different classes in her Sociology program. She reflected. And she learned about the things that didn't "fit" or excite her, and examined every door that opened up for her.

On that cold January morning, she realized that by giving herself freedom and having the guts to take risks and go the opposite direction of her peers after graduation, she became closer to developing her passions at a young age.

See, Nicole didn't have a soul-crushing 9-5 job, as one would expect after graduating college. She used a mix and match approach in the initial months post college to stay in Washington, D.C. and figured it all out while hustling day in and day out. She utilized every connection as well as her creative LinkedIn profile, matched with skill sets she developed along the way in college and her desire to "do the work." This led her to various roles working together with The Niche Movement as well as Social Tables, all while figuring out her likes and dislikes. The most important thing Nicole has learned is to see what's in front of her.

For example, Nicole examined the interviews I compiled over the last 18 months and had the privilege of an early preview to the stories in this book of individuals who have found their niche. I asked her who intrigued her the most and who she would want to connect with. She took me up on the offer and most importantly, she followed through. Within days, she had phone calls and meetings set up to pick the brains of the people in this book and find ways she could help them and open new doors for herself.

From the moment she stepped on American University's campus as a first year student, Nicole talked to everyone. And by no means is she a fearless extrovert. Nicole took risks, sent countless emails, made phone calls and took meetings, all to connect with professionals at places from the Washington Post to the Wedding Wire. It even took her almost 18 months to connect with a coveted event planner, but she prevailed. She kept at it and made it a point to follow up every few months. Negative responses aside, Nicole found ways to stay on the radars of those that inspired her.

It is individuals like Nicole Piquant, like the people in this book, and like those in your own network, that have a caring personality, can-do attitude and limitless drive to not settle that fire me up to help others find their niche.

If I leave you with one message in this book, it is simply this: this is going to be the decade to end employment unhappiness.

The combination of our indefinite, innovative resources to learn new skills, combined with entrepreneurial-sprits and desire to solve problems matched with a world of limitless connection, our generation is set up to not only land exciting jobs but to create the work environments and leadership style we actually enjoy being around every single day. As Nancy Lyons says, it's about "life-balance, not work-life balance."

I'm very stubborn on this subject. In this book, I will walk you through the steps to find your niche and get closer to loving what you do. However, we can't ignore the obvious: finding a job, let alone a job you love, is tough. A 2013 study from Gallup found that 87 percent of workers worldwide and 70 percent of employees in the U.S. are either not engaged or are actively disengaged in the workplace.[i]

If you have ever been through a job search process, you know how time consuming and stressful it can be. Searching and applying for jobs is an exhaustive and an outdated process. And it is a process — a lonely process, at that.

Googling and sifting through stodgy, spam-driven job boards no longer work unless you are just looking for a job versus a career you will thrive in. You spend countless hours either late at night or early in the morning staring at a computer screen. If you're lucky, you find a handful of jobs to apply to. More often than not, your resume goes into an applicant tracking system or online database. You have no human contact and if you are discreetly job searching, you certainly can't express yourself and share with the world. One day of applying becomes one week becomes one month. The next thing you know, you become self-conscious, and doubt sets in. A candidate that is a hard worker, skilled, qualified and inspired to make a difference quickly loses confidence and motivation.

Unfortunately, this on-going cycle cripples the individual and forces them to stay in their current job or company — or if they are lucky enough to get an offer, they hop on the first new job that comes their way. The cycle continues…and so does employment unhappiness.

Origins of The Niche Movement

A lot of my work with The Niche Movement is semi-autobiographical in the sense that the majority of my 20s were spent navigating and discovering the kind of people, leadership and culture that inspire me to do great work. Even though there were times of frustration, disappointment or misaligned values, I now have been able to reflect and find the unseen benefits in the roles and organizations I worked in. More importantly, my values and ability to inspire others around me, especially college students and young professionals, sparked passion and set the north star for The Niche Movement and this book.

The Niche Movement has really been in the works since 2010, but as you will learn in the book, it wasn't until the fall of 2012 that the light bulb went off and I had the clarity around an ever-changing concept to start this movement. In 24 short months, The Niche Movement has been established as a leading community for college students, young professionals, administrators, start-ups and entrepreneurs to connect, share their work and add value to inspire others to find their niche. Through presentations and workshops both in-person and virtually, weekly contributing editor posts and the NicheList — a weekly curated list of jobs 20-somethings will actually love — The Niche Movement is now a community of passionate young professionals that care about ending employment unhappiness for this generation.

How This Book is Organized

This book is organized into nine chapters making up the rules to finding a career path you love. Common themes you will see throughout each chapter revolve around discovering your own strengths and going all in on them. Another theme is realizing that finding your niche may require you to push your comfort zone or continue to evolve and not remain complacent. Lastly, communication has been disrupted. You will read my own stories as it relates to the power of limitless connection, as well as many others' success with breaking through the digital noise in our society.

What You Should Get Out of This Book

This book is written to inspire young professionals and college students (the millennial generation). My goal for this book is to resonate with anyone that is stuck in their life, or in their career and feeling the pressures of being an adult. You could be at the beginning, middle or end of your career and looking for inspiration, optimism and real strategies to find out where you would thrive the most.

First, the stories and strategies in this book will help to provide you with the direction and the clarity that so many people have found through a variety of life and career experiences, both good and bad.

Second, I want you to view this book as an automatic addition to your contact list. Everyone in this book that I wrote about, interviewed or mentioned are down to earth, good people. They are individuals that genuinely want to help others and see others succeed. You will find several of the individuals' websites, Twitter handles or LinkedIn profiles in the back of the book. I recommend that if any of their stories resonate with you and you feel compelled to reach out to them, then please do so. And if I can help facilitate any type of connection, please reach out to me.

Finally, this book will help you reflect on your own personal journey while combining the strategies and resources provided to start discovering your niche and job you love. The number one suggestion as you read this book is to take time to stop and reflect on your own journey. Look at past experiences, be it positive or negative, and find the silver lining that you can take to build upon your strengths. By no means was life easy after I graduated college, and it most certainly took time, effort, adversity and sacrifices to get to where I am today.

Chapter 1

What Does It Mean To Find Your Niche?

When was the last time you were thriving? It may have been running an event, volunteering in a school, facilitating a meeting or playing a sport in high school or college. No matter the scenario, thriving impacts the rest of your life. Whether you are thriving in a classroom, on the field or in the office, the rest of your life is better because of it. I have witnessed many college students thriving on campus, only to graduate and go from thriving to surviving. Surviving is simply settling, and settling sucks. This anomaly doesn't just happen post-graduation — it can happen at just about any stage along the career path. This book is for anyone that wants to find a career in which they can thrive. I call this finding your niche, and I have come to realize that figuring out what that means is the first important step. One of the critical roadblocks facing those that are trying to find their niche is that they don't know which challenges or goals to pursue. They feel lost, and they're overwhelmed by the many possible choices.

In a commencement speech to MIT graduates, Dropbox CEO and founder Drew Houston spoke about the concept of finding your niche. He encouraged graduates to think about the problem they most want to solve in the world and go after it like a dog chasing a tennis ball.[ii] This doesn't have to be some lofty goal. Perhaps you are like Bethany Mota who believed that teenage girls are never taught how to apply make-up the right way, so she created a YouTube channel to solve that problem. You will read about several people in this book similarly to Bethany that have found their niche with big ideas that change the world. You will also read about Francisco Balagtas who has engaged his passion for pizza and Instagram to create a huge following and incredible online presence. No dream or passion is less than any other is, as long as the person on the other end of that dream is thriving. That's what it means to find your niche.

I believe that many people have helped me find my niche, and I want to talk about them in this book. I believe their stories and the ways they impacted my stories can shed light on many different aspects to finding your niche. I'll begin with someone I like to informally refer to as a co-founder of The Niche Movement.

"A lot of women grow up with the dream of getting married and having a child. I think Courtney hit the jackpot because she's getting married to a child."

This is the way John Giannone started out his best man's speech at my wedding. John is the type of guy who can bring laughter to any room. While he is intellectual and hardworking, what I love most about him is his ability to hold a conversation with absolutely anyone. He's a very sarcastic but cerebral guy — the type of guy you always want on your side.

I've known John since we were 3 years old and both attended the same reading hour at our local library in my hometown of Franklin, NJ. Our lives slowly intertwined themselves over the years until our freshman year of high school, when our shared sports teams, classes and mutual friends helped established our friendship that has lasted now into our 30s.

By now, you're probably wondering what John, one of my best friends, has to do with finding your niche? The key is in the relationship.

The best friends that we call family and who are there for us through thick and thin are valuable people in our lives. These relationships build us and shape us, they help us define who we are and they encourage us to find out who we can be. Aside from John's light-hearted and jovial personality, there are a lot of traits that I admire about him. John indirectly played a huge role in the founding of The Niche Movement, the writing of this book that you're holding in your hands and the discovery of my own niche. But there's even more to this story.

John went to Rutgers University, became president of his fraternity, graduated with a degree in Mechanical Engineering and landed a coveted job in his field upon graduation. He has the perfect balance of book smarts and street smarts. He earned his MBA at NYU while working full-time. He's a quick thinker, always offering the perfect punch line to any joke, whether it was told in the boardroom or at the bar.

John is great with family and new friends, always starting conversations with genuine interest to get to know the other person — which is key to a lot of his success. He's great with numbers, contracts, relationship building and does it all while having a natural sense of self-awareness and tact, two skills many (myself included) would love to have at any given moment.

So how did John help influence the Niche Movement? As with many of these stories and new opportunities, it all comes back to timing and being open-minded.

John met an amazing woman, Benee Williams, in August 2012. Now his soon to be wife, Benee has become a staple in John's life, and my life, too. In October 2012, after a Rutgers football game, we invited several friends back to our home in central New Jersey. In the cool, fall air that night, we sat around in the fire pit chatting, and as conversations tend to go, we came to the point where everyone was complaining about their job. At that point, I spoke up and said, "I love my job and get to make a difference in young adult's lives everyday." As you might imagine, I was met with a few strange stares. Enjoy your job? No way. Some of them just didn't get it.

I explained how my greatest passion lies in not only helping college students thrive while they are still in school, but thrive in their 20s after graduation, when the real world sets in. Even though at the time I was the Assistant Director of Digital Media at Rutgers University in the Recreation department, there was something else driving me everyday to work with college students.

I hated seeing talented, hardworking and deserving students who thrived in college come to a screeching halt after graduation. Sometimes it was due to a boss they hated, or a work environment that just wasn't the right fit. Maybe it was a side project they put off, or a graduate program they weren't fully committed to. No matter what their reason was, the truth behind every story I heard was simply that the students and young professionals had no clue what to do. They felt stuck at an average age of 23 years old.

At this point, Benee jumped in, "Kevin, you're trying to help them find their niche!" That is the exact second the light bulb turned on in my head. The next morning, I couldn't stop thinking about her words as I wrote and brainstormed. That evening, I purchased the domain, TheNicheMovement.com. And the rest, as they say, is history.

You know that saying, "Surround yourself with great people" — well, I am lucky to have John Giannone and Benee Williams as close friends. John is one of the very few that I will bounce ideas off of. I know I can tell him accomplishments or new ventures in this journey with The Niche Movement, but he never questions them by saying "what if." He always responds with "That's awesome, man. Let me know how I can help." That is how he inspires me. Its wonderful to know that I have a huge support system as my journey following my passion unfolds.

John taught me to live in the moment, relax and have fun. An idea or project you are working on can come together when you least expect it. Don't be afraid to share your passion with others around you — you never know who will help you up to the next step.

In the first few months after I launched The Niche Movement, I was so excited by the value of sharing my ideas with others that I began blogging on The Niche Movement website. I focused on creating content and adding value, and I wrote a handful of blog posts like "Leadership Lessons from Jay-Z" and "Skip Your Career Fair — 30 Under 30 List." In the beginning, blog posts were infrequent and I only wrote when I had time — a common pitfall for new bloggers and entrepreneurs, as consistency is key.

Looking back on my "How I Found My Niche" series that sparked the writing of this book in summer of 2014, I realized that simply blogging doesn't require more than 45-60 minutes of your time. Sure, the time spent writing day in and day out can add up, but when you have something you are passionate about, the writing (or creating any piece of content) comes easily. It's the amplifying of your words and being heard that's difficult.

In January 2014, a year after launching and building a tribe nationwide, I wanted to provide more content to The Niche Movement's audience. After doing some research, I noticed that sites like the Huffington Post and Post Grad Problems provided content that was built on other contributing editors and bloggers. I realized that on a weekly basis, people that stumbled across The Niche Movement website were seeking help or had an idea that resonated with people searching for employment happiness. I wanted to give others a chance to share their real-world experiences and advice that aligned with the purpose of The Niche Movement.

In less than 6 months, we had 12 contributing editors and a total of 55 blog posts. We established a blogging schedule with one new blog post per week. This tripled our reach and growth.

One of the instrumental forces behind this growth was Amma Marfo, the Assistant Director of Student Activities for Involvement and Assessment at Emmanuel College in Boston, MA. Amma deeply believes that young adults should be encouraged to find a career path that suits each individual's skills and talents — exactly what The Niche Movement wants for you, too.

Amma penned a series for us called "See What Sticks." One of my favorite blog posts in her series is "Questlove's Guide to Success at the Office." In this post, Amma recapped Questlove's story for his love of music that has translated into a love of life and career advice. The most important piece of advice to remember from her post is that it may not be your first job out of college that will allow you to build your masterpiece, but you will learn skills that will help you create your vision in the future.

After reading and sharing posts like this one with our audience, I decided to create a Contributing Editor position where others could use The Niche Movement as a venue to inspire and share their stories. It is people like Amma who brought this platform to the next level.

There are many skills that the people in this book have in common, but the most important qualities you will see that thread them together are that they are connectors, insightful and genuinely care about other's success and happiness.

I invited Amma to share some of her best advice with you. During her interview, we talked about introversion in relation to networking and job searching. Amma shared that, in her experience, people who are introverted are generally great at listening and storing information away for future use. If you consider yourself introverted, take advantage of this skill and use it to propel you ahead while in interviews and in networking settings. You remember details easily, which can aid you in building a strong relationship and establishing a connection with those around you. People love to be appreciated, and you are in the best position to appreciate them.

As this book introduces you to others who have found their niche and are thriving, you will see how an idea that was created with a passion for helping college students and young professionals has grown into what it is today. The Niche Movement really began with the meetings in my office with students who needed career advice. It grew when I would go to a campus and speak to students, and increased when I had our first virtual cohort. However, adding this component of contributing bloggers has amplified the message in ways I could have never done alone.

If you have a passion for something or a vision, don't rely solely on yourself to execute that vision. Find ways to include others in the process and you will not only create opportunities for others, but most importantly, they will bring new life and diverse perspectives to the table. Your audience will appreciate the well-rounded content you provide. A movement may start with one person, but it only gains the momentum necessary to create change with the help of others.

We all want a career path that we choose and that is not chosen for us. We want a path that aligns with our passions, talents and strengths. Over the course of our life, our passions and strengths can change, which can often influence our career interests. I can still remember being 7 years old; all I did was play with Legos and Pipeworks. Yes, I'm a 90s kid brought up on Full House and the evolution of dial-up Internet.

Many children get excited just dumping hundreds of Legos across their living room and watching their parents clean them up. But for me, it was more than that. I became enthralled with the process of constructing, and what I loved the most was knowing that whatever I built was solely mine. Arriving at the finished product of the Lego toy pictured on the box came easy to me. Little did I realize that this pleasure, where my imagination soared boundlessly, would be the first of many passions that would begin to influence my life and feed my quest to realize who I am and what I could do when I grew up.

If you were to ask me what I wanted to do with the rest of my life during the Lego years, I would have said to become an engineer or architect.

However, after picking up my first golf club a few years later, and subsequently falling in love with the game during my freshman year of high school, I traded Legos for drivers and putters.

If you were to ask me again in high school where my life was headed, I would have said a "PGA Director of Golf."

After being inspired by great teachers and coaches in high school, I went on to college, but not to become a Director of Golf. Because I was shy and somewhat introverted, I wanted a small school no more than a few hours from home. Fortunately, I was accepted to Fairleigh Dickinson University

(FDU) and made the Division III golf team where I played collegiate golf all four years.

If you were to ask me again at the beginning of my college career, what I would do in life, I would have said a teacher.

Do you remember when you were a child or in high school headed into college?

What were your career goals then?

How does that match up with your vision now?

Everyone has these moments and transitions of "life plans." From kindergarten-age to the present, society has continued to ask, "What do you want to do when you grow up?" For most of us, we are still asked this question by others, and more often than not, by our own conscience.

In this book, you will read more about my journey and the stories of others that helped shape that journey. Think of these stories as kaleidoscopes, vivid colors with outcomes that become more intricate, beautiful and developed with a simple change of direction or pivot. These people have truly inspired me and have lent great influence to my life that will help shape and bring clarity to your career journey, too.

This book is an account of the heroes, influencers and inspirational stories of those who are navigating life at all ages, and who have found their niche along the way. They are the people who love what they do. This is about the people that inspired me, motivated me, picked me up when I was down, told me to take a risk and told me I was a leader. They helped me inch closer to finding my niche, and their stories can do the same for you.

These people are all empathetic and kind individuals, with unique personalities and unbridled passion for their respective crafts. I am proud to give you an authentic glimpse into their journeys to find their niche, as these people are inspiring and represent the new rules for finding a career you love.

The older we get, the more obvious it becomes that our families played an important role in shaping us into the adults we are today. So much of our upbringing and experiences during those early years influences our values and passions later in the life.

In my late 20s and now early 30s, I've found myself counting my blessings — I feel lucky to have both my parents, Kevin and Mary, alive and healthy and by my side. It is astonishing to see how much their characteristics, values and personalities have influenced my growth and are reflected in who I am at 32 years old.

My father, Kevin, is the hardest working, most caring and selfless man I know. He's reserved, soft-spoken and conservative. My mom, Mary, on the other hand, is the life of the party, could talk a dog off a bone and has the sharpest memory I've ever witnessed (this has its pros and cons, believe me).

I get my hardworking, help everyone attitude from my dad, but I also use my mom's charm to strike up conversations, network and connect to people. But on top of that, I'm most grateful that the "memory gene" has been passed onto me from my great grandmother. I can't tell you how beneficial it has been when building relationships with everyone I meet and reconnecting with those I haven't seen in a while.

Growing up, my parents were able to strike a balance between living a simple life, while still leaving room for the ability to dream and try something new. I know they want me to be happy. I never felt any pressure that my parents had a black and white definition of what success looks like.

The word success is subjective and something that constantly changes. From an early age, my parents also let me make my own path and grow my own way, along with guidance and support as expected from parents. I was never pressured to follow a family member's footsteps or pressured to do anything I didn't want to do. They allowed me to be who I wanted to be and when I reached out for help, they were always there.

Most importantly, they taught me that there's always a way to make it work. Whether it relates to finances, marriage, family or a career, with perspective, you can find a way to solve the problem, move forward and look to the bright side.

There is someone out there that has shaped your life — past, present, or future:

1. Don't take them for granted.
2. Consider how they've inspired you and pass that message onto others.
3. If you desperately want something, find a way to make it work.

Chapter Two

Know Yourself and Embrace It

People who use their strengths every day are six times more likely to be engaged on the job.[iii] Your ability to use your strengths every day in your job relies on a variety of factors. Most individuals that are utilizing their strengths every day are working in a job that is aligned with those strengths and talents, in addition to working for a supervisor that intentionally aligns projects and assignments to this. The question remains, what do you do if you don't know your strengths? Part of finding a job or a project that matches the sweet spot for you is based on your ability to be self-aware and understand your strengths. This chapter will shed light on the stories of many people that continue to learn about themselves and put that knowledge to use in hopes of finding their niche.

I remember it like it was yesterday: I was halfway through my spring semester of sophomore year of college and my girlfriend Courtney suggested I apply to become an orientation leader at FDU. She, of course, had already applied.

My first reaction to her suggestion was, "Oh, she just wants me to apply so we don't have to be away from each other during the summer." To this day, I still believe that, but she also had the foresight that a) I was qualified, b) it would change me for the better and c) I would be a great role model for Fairleigh Dickinson's incoming students. Well, I hate to admit it, but she was right — on every count.

Needless to say, Courtney, 16 others and myself went on to become FDU's 2004 Orientation Leaders. That summer changed my life for the better. Becoming an orientation leader has been one of the biggest risks I have taken to date. While this may seem silly to the extrovert that loves to speak in front of others, this was a terrifying leap into uncharted territory for a painstakingly shy guy like me.

The summer between my sophomore and junior year in college, I pushed myself out of my comfort zone and didn't move back home to my parents house for the summer. Instead, I stayed on campus and began working as an orientation leader. Going into this six-week program, I had no idea what I was getting into. At the time, I didn't realize what this experience would bring and the critical point that would shift my future let alone take my college career from good to great.

I vividly remember my first-year orientation at FDU and Mark Bullock, my orientation leader, saying, "The more you put into college, the more you'll get out of it."

During my first two years in college, I didn't quite understand what Mark met by that statement.

However, that summer when I stayed on campus and did something unconventional from my friends, Mark's statement began to have meaning. Immediately, I had 15 new friends that summer, all living together in a string of suites at FDU. Our group of orientation leaders were inseparable: we worked 10-12 hour days together, played volleyball after work, went to concerts together and behaved like typical college students who had a campus all to themselves during the summer.

Growing up as a shy child, I finally felt like I was putting myself out there and coming out of my shell. I suddenly had several groups of friends with who I felt like I could be myself around. During this time, and unbeknownst to me, I was becoming a leader. Waking up early on my own and taking initiative to set up tables in the student center without being asked: check. Running icebreakers in front of groups of 18 year olds by myself: check. Learning to work with several different types of personalities: check. And last but not least: performing on stage in front of hundreds of first year students twice a week: check!

FDU's orientation was led by Sarah Azavedo (Director of Student Life) with Ray Flook and Nathalie Waite (both Assistant Directors). One morning, Sarah wanted to meet with me early before that day's sessions. I, of course, thought I was headed to the boss' office because I had done something wrong.

Turns out, that wasn't the case; she told me there was a student named Anna attending that day's session that had a disability. She wanted me to be at her side for the next 48 hours to make her feel welcomed, help her get around campus and connect her with other peers. Half of me was terrified. The other half was shouting, "Yes, I'll do it!" in my head.

Well the adrenaline kicked in, I said yes, willing to push the boundaries of my comfort zone. I met Anna early that morning. She was just two years younger than me and her energy and personality were exhilarating and downright contagious. She was so excited to be at college and meet new people — she couldn't get enough of it. Later that day, I met up with Courtney, who had a 30-minute break. She joined Anna and I, and we had the privilege to give her a private tour of campus.

That was when we really got to know Anna.

It turns out Anna was in a car accident when she was younger and had to rely on a wheelchair to get around. She also had a slight speech impediment. But what I saw was a young girl with a lot of ambition and enthusiasm for life. I really feel like she came out of her shell because we treated her as we would any other incoming student. It was one of the most rewarding days that summer, and Courtney and I still reminisce about that day.

At this point about halfway through the summer program, I started to become more self-aware and realized I had a special new skill set. We could insert the word leader here; however, that word never entered my mind as a way to describe myself. What I realized is Sarah saw that I was a compassionate and a thoughtful young individual that was trustworthy. Most importantly, she saw potential in me.

What happened next was the real tipping point for me, and it had a major influence on my career path and finding my niche.

Twelve orientation sessions later, summer came to an end. After a short two-week break, I was back on campus to start the second half of my college career. It was the first week of September and Sarah, Ray and Nat scheduled one-on-ones with each orientation leader to provide feedback about the summer and get suggestions for the next year's orientation class. I didn't know what to expect, and went into the meeting very timidly.

However, my attitude quickly changed. I sat there; my bosses asked me, "Kevin, do you know you are a leader?" I was shocked at what they said and I answered the question, "No, I never saw myself as a leader." No one had ever said that to me before.

When they said that, though, my whole outlook on life changed and something clicked for me. I started to have confidence in myself, to take more calculated risks and to not be afraid to put myself out there. This conversation was a pivotal time and my outlook on life hasn't been the same since that moment.

The best thing is that Nathalie demonstrated her belief in my potential yet again years later into my professional career. In both 2014 and 2015, she invited me to present at a leadership workshop to international graduate students from all around the world at Steven's Institute of Technology, knowing I could adapt and connect with a diverse audience.

Ray, Nat and Sarah saw my potential. They saw something in me, and more importantly, shared what they saw with me. As I became more involved during my junior and senior year, my outlook on life turned into something completely different than my perspective as a timid new student on campus.

If you are an educator, leader or even supervisor, don't let an opportunity to tell someone that they are a leader pass you by. My life would have been vastly different if they never told me about their perception of me in that one meeting. Even if they were thinking it, I would never have known unless they said something. Always take the moment to say something when you have the chance.

We are often our own toughest critics, and we tend to put ourselves in boxes. For instance, during the early part of my life, I put myself in the "shy kid" box. I've seen students put themselves in the "not good at school" box, the "introverted" box and so on. It is said that we often put ourselves and others into categories, often resulting in stereotypes, because our brain will look for cognitive shortcuts.[iv]

With all the information we have to remember, our brain will create shortcuts to make it easier for us to remember or make sense of everything going on in the world around us. Unfortunately, this often leads to the "boxes" to which I am referring. Look outward for help on finding your niche. Ask others what they see in you. You may be surprised to hear what your supervisor, mentor or friends think of you.

Recent studies have proven that employees who feel engaged in their work are more productive, profitable, stay longer and produce a higher quality work.[v] The employment happiness factor influences many other aspects of your work and life. This kind of engagement can often peak our curiosity and encourage us to explore new terrain. That is exactly what happened to Noah Rosenberg, and it resulted in an incredible storytelling movement.

When Noah Rosenberg's kindergarten teacher assigned him a sentence assignment, she wasn't expecting lengthy, complex run-ons from the little boy. Even at the tender age of 5, Noah knew he enjoyed playing with words, stringing them together to make dynamic prose. Noah's love for writing followed him throughout high school, where he wrote for the school newspaper, and into college, where he became a reporter for Tufts Daily and various literary magazines. In addition to being involved in the literary community, Noah also worked with video, creating a documentary that captured the fervent 2004 presidential campaign happening in and around Boston. This experience taught Noah the power of video storytelling.

After graduation, Noah's career took off. During his days off from his job at CBS Productions and, later, The Queens Courier, Noah would do some reporting on the side, engaging swimmers from New York City's Polar Bear Club and writing other human-interest articles to satisfy his craving for storytelling. In 2008, Noah realized that traditional media outlets, like newspapers, were disappearing. He began looking for ways to keep elements of the publications alive — stories that detail the human condition, instead of being about pop culture, politics or entertainment and have greater, wider appeal.

The variety of assignments Noah had, ranging from South Africa, where Noah covered the World Cup, to places like GQ Magazine, Univision and the New York Times helped him develop the skills that would ultimately help him build his dream. Noah followed ideas that spoke to his passion and kept "doing what he thought was important and what would pay off in the end." In 2010, Noah contacted a few of his friends within the industry to hammer out ideas for a website. In September 2012, Narratively launched.

Noah feels that he would not have been able to launch his creating without building a list of contacts. People are now able to build a following through their computer — take advantage of it! Though meeting someone face-to-face is always the best way to establish a connection, technological tools are also at our quick disposal. Reach out to those that you admire and see how you can help them. Try to cultivate an invaluable team of people around you who can help you. You want them to put in just as much blood, sweat and tears as you do.

Though contacting those who influence you can be the first step in establishing a powerful relationship, it's imperative that you master the art of the email. Be sure to explain who you are, why the influencer should be paying attention to you and explain what you can offer them.

Public speaking skills are also essential for college students looking for jobs, and they aren't necessarily always used at a podium. They come in handy when you're interacting with someone at a bar, a networking event or a college career fair. The ability to look someone in the eye and tell someone what you're all about, why they need you and what you need from them is paramount. Basically, you need to be able to shape your own story. It's important to tell people what your mission is.

Finally, always follow your dreams. Of course money is important, but try to find the place where finances and your passion meet. Every experience is a building block. Try to take a lesson from each of your experiences, whether it was positive or negative. Each job and internship gives you insight into what you do and do not like.

Noah Rosenberg continued to follow his passion until it led him to create a renowned platform that publishes unsung heroes from across the globe. The company is constantly looking for people to pitch ideas and those with marketing, business development and social media skills.

When we read a story like Noah's, it can trigger emotions associated with being inspired and excited for the future. It can also make us feel frustrated. Deep down we may be thinking, "When will I ever get my big break?" If that's what you are thinking, don't be ashamed. It is completely natural for us to compare our stories to others and to often get frustrated with how far we have to go to achieve our biggest ambitions. It may make you feel better to know that you are not alone.

A recent study tracked the ages of Nobel Prize winners, great innovators and scientists and the researchers found a groundbreaking theme connecting the individuals involved in the study. Their most revolutionary work peaked during their late 30s — at least 10 years into any individual career.[vi] Since many of us are changing our careers so often these days, you can't even really use your 30s as a benchmark. The lesson is that many successful leaders and influencers go about 10 years with very little recognition before they hit their creative breakthrough.

So, what do you do while you are working your way through those 10 or so years until your big break? Let your talents and skills speak for themselves and keep pushing forward. I learned this when I was playing golf in high school.

Like you, I have had many vital life experiences that have profoundly shaped who I am today. One of these was a weeklong trip to England and Wales I took with my golf team in high school. When the opportunity arose, my parents didn't hesitate to say, "Yes, Kevin go!" This trip turned out not only to be one of the best golf trips I have ever been on, but a cultural experience that let me see the world for the first time outside of the United States.

Who was the driving force behind this trip? The one and only legend from my high school: Mike Harris, the Wallkill Valley High School's golf coach and history department head. Mr. Harris, along with a friend who lived in England, was a catalyst for this experience and created a weeklong exchange program with golf teams from the U.K.

Now, Mr. Harris isn't one of my influencers just because he coordinated one of the most memorable trips of my life. Even though I didn't have him as a teacher in a classroom, he built upon the values and lessons my parents instilled in me. He taught me so much, both on and off the golf course — both about golf and about life.

The first year I tried out for the golf team, I didn't make the cut. Instead of quitting in favor of something else, coming up short spurred me to work to be a better golfer. I hit thousands of balls between those two years and finally made the team my sophomore year. After my JV debut, I shot somewhere north of 60 on nine holes (in case you don't play golf, an average of 39 is considered a good score in a nine-hole competitive round of high school golf). Instead of giving up on me, Mr. Harris believed in me. He continued to give me chances, pushed me to be better and gave me the space I needed to see what I was capable of.

My senior year, I was playing in the fourth spot for varsity and our team wound up winning the county championship. Throughout my entire career playing on Mr. Harris' golf team, he constantly encouraged us to go about our business day by day, to not get too confident and focus on our own work. Even though I believed we deserved more recognition for our accomplishments that year, he told us to let our scores, personality and sportsmanship on the golf course do the talking.

Today, Mr. Harris is still a social studies teacher and the golf coach at my high school. He is still encouraging young adults to keep trying until they can see what they are capable of. He is still living the same lesson he taught me all those years ago — be humble, continue to grind and improve, because when you are good at what you do, people will notice and your talents will speak for themselves. This life advice more than 15 years later sticks with me and keeps me grounded through the wins and losses in my professional life.

Steve Jobs is famous for saying, "people with passion can change the world for the better."[vii] There is a surprising amount of controversy over whether people should follow their passion in their careers. Some say that following your passion is terrible advice because it won't lead to a lucrative career.[viii] Others argue that when a job activates someone's passion, everyone wins, as it has a positive impact on the employee and can lead to higher profits for the company.[ix] This is why I appreciate and use the phrase "finding your niche." It encompasses passion, strengths and overall employment happiness. This next story truly brings Steve Jobs' quote to life by giving it a story that we can all relate to.

Nathan Resnick is not your typical college junior. He's already started several successful Kickstarter campaigns, including one for his own company, Yes Man Watches. He goes cliff jumping with his friends in between classes at the University of San Diego. He considers himself an entrepreneur, and works hard each day to achieve his dreams.

Hailing from Bethesda, MD, Nathan has always had an entrepreneurial spirit. While working 9 to 5 at his sales internship, he came across an unusual, yet cool-looking belt design that caught his eye. He wondered whether the design could also be applied to a watch. Nathan began drafting plans for the watch, working on a website and asking friends about a slogan. Within 5 months, Nathan had launched a Kickstarter campaign. Yes Man Watches, he says, not only tell time, but help people consider their *use* of time.

"Everyone has 24 hours in a day," Nathan says, "and going to a 9 to 5 job is only one third of your day. That gives you plenty more time to achieve your goals."

Try to set short-term goals to achieve your long-term ones. With each completed objective, you'll get closer and closer to your dream. Apps also help you consider your use of time. One of Nathan's favorites is Stay Focused, a plugin that limits the amount of time you go on specific websites of your choosing. He acknowledges that procrastination is rampant on college campuses, saying that when he goes to the library, nearly half of everyone there is on Instagram, Twitter or Facebook. Instead, he says, it helps to be results driven. It helps when you get the opportunity to revel in the fruits of your labor. It also helps to have your hand in several different projects to fight boredom.

Having a strong interest in the projects you're working on is also key to its success. "Passion is the fuel that keeps your fire going," Nathan says. You won't want to do the things that are required when starting your own business, like having super early mornings and extremely late nights without it. Perseverance is the second skill that's necessary when trying to get your project off of the ground. Many people will deny you access, say they don't like your idea or say you shouldn't pursue your dream. You have to continue moving forward despite the challenges. Traveling, trying new things and exploring are all things that can help you find your passion. Personally, Nathan says, the classes he's passionate about are the ones in which he's more inclined to learn, do the readings and get papers in on time.

When thinking about a new idea, entering business planning competitions are a great way to determine the worth of your project. Many schools and incubators offer them — students simply get a team together and plan out their business model or create a prototype for it. Winners often receive money to help launch their business, and receive mentors and entrepreneurship training. Having contacts and networking is also essential to getting your idea out into the real world. After contacting 20 people, Nathan admits, only five people will respond, and one will actually help him out. Follow up with people, and stay in contact with them even before you need to utilize the connections.

There's a strong possibility that, when you're just starting out, you'll be working on many different projects by yourself. "There's no such thing as 'intern work,'" Nathan has found. Everything is important and valuable, and nothing is beneath you. However, when it comes time to outsource certain projects, check out websites like Upwork and Freelance. However, be sure to cross-reference people who offer to work for you. Find out whether they have their own website, have been to tradeshows and if they have a social media presence. You want to be sure that they are truly who they say they are before you hire them.

Many entrepreneurs can only dream of the success that Nathan Resnick had in less than a year of launching his business. He writes for Entrepreneur.com and been featured in The Bro Bible and Bloomberg Businessweek, in addition to running Yes Man Watches and adding a sunglasses to his product line. It is evident that Nathan Resnick is surely a young entrepreneur to watch as he continues to fulfill his dreams and chase his passions.

Some people, like Nate, know exactly what they are passionate about. They understand how to activate those passions and attract others to turn those passions into movements, organizations or companies. However, most of us need a little help learning about ourselves. As you can remember from the beginning of this chapter, I struggled with this a great deal in college. Shauna Rubin-Murphy's story and the tips she provides in this next section offer some clarity to those that may be struggling with this.

Shauna niche lies in the non-profit sector. It has taken her five years since she graduated from college to get to a point in her career where she is beyond happy and feels that she is in the right place. There was a year within those five years where she worked for a small non-profit in New Jersey. The work overall was fulfilling; however, the management of the organization and those who she worked for made her job miserable, unsatisfying and at the end of the day, she questioned her whole career. Shauna became overwhelmed, stressed, depressed and didn't make time for family or friends and even herself.

Luckily, Shauna moved on from the organization and after the rollercoaster of job searching again, she found a job working for a corporate foundation that she now loves.

She is a much stronger and happier person since moving on. She now has a boss that gives her autonomy and is letting her grow professionally under her management. In her own words, "I can truly call her a mentor."

Now, what do you do when you are in a bad work situation with a bad boss and how do you go about moving on and looking for a new job? Here are five tips to think about when you find yourself in a similar situation as Shauna and ways to avoid it all together.

1. Let your emotions make you stronger

There can be days or weeks where you are frustrated, angry and emotionally or physically drained. Use these emotions to make yourself stronger. If you need to cry, cry. If you need to take yourself out of a situation, take yourself out. Turn your emotions into useful energy. Make a list of things or reasons that make you feel this way and turn them into interview questions or as pros/cons when job searching. If you get to a breaking point, schedule time for yourself, even for just an hour a day to do something you enjoy can make a world of difference when you are unhappy at work.

2. The grass can be greener on the other side (if you let it be)

This is not how this quote usually goes; however, there are reasons why you're unhappy with your job or the way management treats you. When it comes to reasons to leave a job, you need to think about your strengths and weaknesses.

If you left your current position, what can you bring to the table in your new position? Also, think about all the reasons why you felt unhappy with management at your previous job and how you define good management. Being respected, having similar work values and expectations can make all the difference when having a good manager.

3. Look at any challenge as a learning experience, not a regret

Everything you learned can be a resume builder or a good answer to some tough interview questions. You want to take any challenge and turn it into a positive. Be proactive as much as you can. As miserable as you are or however bad a day is, there are always learning experiences and professional development. Whatever you can take with you, gain as much experience as possible. You will look back one day and be happy you went through the experience.

4. Look for red flags during the interview

You can leave an interview feeling as if it was your greatest you've ever had; however, take time to analyze how it went. Make sure that you got a complete idea of what the culture, employee engagement, moral and management styles are like. Craft questions about these areas and try to get a sense of the organization or company. Follow up with the person who interviewed you and ask some of these questions if you didn't get a chance to during the interview. Really think about the questions you were asked. Were you asked about your strengths and weaknesses, future goals, your idea of a good work environment and how you can contribute to the company or organization? Paying attention to red flags can save you from a job that would be unsuitable for you.

5. Always have your own back.

Never let management or your boss's behavior become an excuse for you. When you are in a very unhappy situation and you are looking for a way out, only you can make that change. Create or re-look at your personal and professional network, talk to as many people who you trust and see how your network can help you change positions and find new opportunities. Try to take the high road as much as possible and continue to be professional until you are able to move on.

This all takes time. It takes a great deal of reflection, and good people around you. Some people have used alternative strategies such as meditation, practicing yoga or even taking time to do some traveling in order to engage in this self-reflection process. Be patient, and know that there are many people like Shauna that want to help. Never hesitate to reach out and ask for strategies or tips.

When you have found your niche, you tend to be very good at your job. As you build a reputation for doing good work, you will most likely get a little more autonomy and flexibility. Perhaps you can choose your projects or the people you work with. You want to leverage this by investing in more projects that align with your purpose and personality.

Over the course of my post-college life as a young professional working more than eight years in the Student Affairs field, I have been lucky enough to work on several amazing projects with talented students and colleagues that I am in constant awe of.

One of these people is also undeniably one of the most incredible people I've ever had the pleasure of meeting while working at Rutgers University. Both because of her working philosophy and because she can deliver a T-shirt cannon to me for an event with less than four hours' notice. #TrueStory

Her name is Carey Loch, and she's the Director of Programs for Rutgers Student Life, but her job title is just the beginning of who she really is. Carey is the driving force behind some of the most successful programs at Rutgers, including Dance Marathon, Beats on the Bank, and all of Homecoming week, including the legendary Bed Races (and these are just the big-ticket events).

Not only is Carey a colleague in Student Affairs and a close friend, but she is someone I look up to because she brings both the product and the punch to the party, the office, the Build-A-Thon — wherever she's headed on any given day. Through genuine hard work, she has established thriving collaborative relationships with several departments that come together to bring the "wow" factor to typically normal college events. Carey has created partnerships that have been indispensable to the programming offered to Rutgers students. She has built a legacy and continues to positively shape the experiences of Rutgers students.

Have I mentioned yet that she does all of this with one of the brightest and most positive personalities I've ever witnessed? Because of this, she is often rewarded with more work and more people wanting to work with her. So how does she do it? Who does she decide to say "yes" to and what to say "no" to?

It's simple — she has one trifold philosophy: Principle. Product. Personality.

Principle:
When she starts a project or partners with someone, she wants to make sure everyone involved is doing it for the right reason. In a field dedicated to helping college students, the

principle she is looking for is generally for the students or for the college community.

Ask yourself: Do the people you're working with share in your vision and believe in your goals?

Product:
For Carey, producing a quality project is a huge value for her, especially if her name is going to be associated with it. When she is working with others, she wants to make sure these people will walk the walk, instead of just talking about it.

Ask yourself: Will the people around me be as invested in the outcome as I am?

Personality:
Her personality is contagious and anyone that gets to associate with her is lucky. In that regard, the third part of her philosophy is clear — you better play nice in the sandbox. She knows that not everyone may be as upbeat as she is, but you should be optimistic, able to carry a conversation and share similar values while leaving the politics at your office door. Also, it doesn't hurt if you like to have a good time while you work.

Ask yourself: Are you working with optimists that you can rely on no matter the circumstance?

Even though the events Carey puts together are large scale and draw significant attention, many times her work largely goes unnoticed. Remember, a genius often goes a long time before getting any recognition, but she's okay with that. Like many people we have met so far, she is selfless and chooses to focus on the bigger picture. The more you realize your life and career is a marathon and not a sprint to get ahead and remain patient, trusting that good things will come, the greater your chances for success and for good karma to come your way.

Part of finding your niche is having the ability to know yourself and embracing it. It may be learning your passions and finding jobs to activate them, or like Carey, aligning projects with your principles and purpose. Reflection is the secret weapon used by just about every person featured in this book. They all found their niche and engage in the ever-evolving process of career exploration because they possess excellent self-reflection skills. Part of knowing you is also knowing your comfort zone. You will need to know the boundaries of your comfort zone — as we are about to find out, life and your niche begins at the edge of your comfort zone.

Chapter 3
Take Risks and Dive Into Discomfort

Your comfort zone is a behavioral space that provides a state of mental security because your activities and behaviors fit a routine that minimizes stress and/or risk.[x] We are drawn to stay within our comfort zone because there are lower levels of stress and anxiety about the unknown associated with this space. However, we are less creative and productive in our comfort zone. The lack of urgency that is often associated with the unknown results in lower productivity. You know that feeling of being on your toes? You are alert and ready to solve problems. We lose that feeling in our comfort zone. In addition, we only seek information that we already agree with while we are in our comfort zone. This inhibits our creativity and curiosity — two traits we see each person in this book exhibit at least once in their story.

The truth is that we will stay in a job we hate because it's comfortable and because we have a fear of the unknown. How can something we hate be considered comfortable? Think about it. While our boss might drive us nuts, we know that we can live off the salary provided. We know the shortcuts necessary to finish the day by 4:30pm, or the ways to avoid the annoying co-worker. The known, even if it's bad, is often seen as being better than the unknown. We stay in these jobs, come home frustrated and angry and live in this perpetual cycle of figuring out ways to just deal with it. The truth is that our fear of failure is probably our biggest obstacle to growth. When we were kids we had no fears. Our curiosity and lack of fear led to many adventures and accelerated growth.

As you will read in this chapter, life and employment happiness almost always can be found outside of your comfort zone. The risk-takers are rewarded with adventures driven by their passions. I've learned that if you don't look out for yourself, no one else will. You must take ownership over your destiny. When you are ready to dive into discomfort and truly open yourself up to all the good and bad that may come along with that, you will be handsomely rewarded with infinite possibilities.

After 13 years (including five plus years of marriage), my wife Courtney still knows what's good for me even when I don't see it myself. She knows how to motivate me, offer encouragement when I need it and pick me back up when I'm at rock bottom. I thank her for that. Her work ethic has always amazed me, but scared me at the same time. When she finds something that she is passionate about, she goes all in and will do whatever it takes to get it done. And that's what I love about being able to spend the rest of my life with her.

Courtney and I have the ability to feed off of each other's success to propel the other even further ahead. It's very similar to NASCAR "drafting" — two cars moving nose to tail can go faster than two cars side by side. The more ambitious either of us is, we always find a way to keep up, tailing right behind one another. When I see Courtney's hard work pay off, I see the value of the hustle I've been putting in and know it will all be worth the work and effort.

My wife has quite a head on her shoulders. At an early stage in her career, she has already racked up numerous awards and recognition within her industry, planned a national education conference, given two TEDx talks and is a Huffington Post contributing editor. Aside from her work ethic and skill sets, she has an uncanny ability to put others ahead of herself and go the extra mile for them or for the project at hand.

I'm fortunate to have someone like her to bounce ideas off of and receive help when I ask. My wife has made a huge impact on me. She has always seen the light at the end of the tunnel, helped me solve problems in both work and my personal life and encourages me to see the optimistic side of things. Courtney has taught me I need to find the silver lining in all that I do and to be the most positive and proactive version of myself. Overall, she has taught me not to give up on my dreams, big or small. If someone you trust and that knows you well suggests you try something or put yourself out there, listen to them. Take that leap of faith. Push yourself out of your comfort zone. When you find a person you can be in the foxhole with, day in and day out, don't let them go — work hard as hell to keep them in your life!

When you are diving into discomfort like Courtney often is, you tend to be a perpetual rookie. On July 26, 2013, Courtney received a job offer to work for Erik Qualman, a prominent thought leader and author on digital leadership. She didn't even think there was a job title in the offer. She didn't need one, because she knew it was an incredible opportunity she had to take. Fast-forward about four weeks and she headed up to Boston for her first few days in her new job. The first day on the job, Erik and Courtney went to a marketing conference. She can still remember Erik handing her nametag to her and it said "Socialnomics Chief of Development." She later posted a picture of the nametag on Facebook, with a status that read, "Well I guess I need to figure out what a Chief of Development does."

The next day, Erik showed her a spreadsheet he set up for the team to organize the publishing process for his next book. Courtney remembers looking at the spreadsheet and feeling like it was in a different language. She was terrified. She had no clue that business development was even a thing, and her first assignment felt like it was written in a foreign language.

Running parallel to her journey into the unknown of business development and publishing was some new interest in her ideas around education. Right before starting with Equalman Studios, Courtney gave a TEDx talk on August 4, 2013 about going all in on innovation in education. All of a sudden, people wanted to talk more about her ideas. In her eyes, she was completely unqualified to be an education expert — even though she has a master's degree in higher education and has worked in the field for 10 years. However, she couldn't turn down the opportunities and new connections that could potentially create change and help students.

So there she was...fully removed from everything she knew, starting her rookie year. The following are four lessons Courtney learned from her experiences and shares pulling from Liz Wiseman's *Rookie Smarts* as a framework. Wiseman identifies the four mindsets of rookies: Backpacker, Hunter-Gatherer, Firewalker and the Pioneer. Those mindsets resonated with Courtney and served as a way to organize her thoughts on this rookie year. The following is a piece she wrote for the book to describe this experience and the lessons we can all learn from it.

The Backpacker's Approach to Publishing a Book

It was day five in the new job and I was home from Boston looking at that spreadsheet that felt like it was written in gibberish. I decided that the first thing I needed to do was learn everything I could about publishing. I read every blog post, eBook and article I could get my hands on about publishing. I bookmarked the crap out of all the resources I found. I had poster boards filled with Post-its noting various options for distribution channels, royalty options and marketing programs. I scoured the terrain quickly and freely. Not to mention, I had all the confidence in the world coming from Erik. He just kept saying, "You're going to be one of the most knowledgeable people in the world about this process!" It was only a matter of time before I knew enough to not only fill in that spreadsheet Erik created, but also to felt confident enough to explain my findings to Erik and the team.

Wiseman explains in *Rookie Smarts* that rookies have nothing to weigh them down. The years of experience and accolades that most veterans possess are great, but can often cause them to act like caretakers of the status quo. Backpackers only have a light bag of essentials on their back, and so they can explore new terrain freely. I backpacked my way through the artisan publishing process. At the end of my first rookie year, I can proudly say that the book was published in time for holiday sales and we've sold over 10,000 copies in the first nine months!

The Hunter-Gatherer Does Disruption in Education

Most experts in education have been working in education reform for years. Here I was with seven years of experience and passion for making education a better experience for students. As people approached me to speak at their event or in their classes about innovating education, I would graciously accept. Each opportunity gave me more chances to ask the audience questions, and hunt down more experts to get their thoughts on how I could improve upon my ideas. In November, I started publishing blogs on HuffPost EDU. I got my first dose of negative comments on blast! I had to embrace the vulnerability, and channel my inner hunter-gatherer. Each negative comment was an opportunity to learn what I needed to change about how I was communicating my ideas. Alternatively, it was an opportunity to learn a new side of the story that would in turn help me beef up my expertise.

Wiseman classifies this type of approach as the hunter-gatherer mindset. Rookies know they don't know everything, so they act much like a caveman looking for food and building a shelter. We hunt for expertise and believe it can come from anywhere and in any form. Each new interaction is an opportunity to contribute to our growing foundation and ideas. As my first rookie year comes to an end, I have embraced my new opportunity to inspire change in education. I have spoken at several different events, wrote a blog for HuffPost EDU on the habits of innovative educators that was shared over 3,000 times and I continue to learn from each experience.

Firewalking My Way Through Business Development

It took me some time, but I finally figured out what a business development person does…they bring in new business opportunities! I had no experience or training on how one generates new leads or how to identify potential business opportunities. At first, I wanted to treat it like the publishing process, and spend time exploring and learning the terrain. However, I quickly realized I didn't have the luxury of spending months learning the process; I needed to move quicker than that. I would need to walk on the hot coals and learn through each encounter. I paid close attention to Erik and the team's interactions with clients. I would try to send some cold emails to potential new clients and then when I never heard back, I would quickly get feedback from the team and send a follow-up. I came up with ways to merge my expertise and connections in education with the work our team was doing. This turned out to be a winning combination.

The rookie is cautious and quick just like a firewalker. In *Rookie Smarts*, Wiseman talks about how our knowledge gap forces us to talk to people and seek feedback often. Instead of going down a long path with little insight or feedback, rookies take quick trips over the hot coals and then seek out feedback on areas to improve. After a few months, I am still very much firewalking my way through. However, I did start to find my stride in the last 60 days after closing a few big contracts. Not only is it a great feeling to create new business, but it's even better when you believe whole-heartedly in what you're selling.

Pioneering to Reach More Educators

In April, I spoke to a division of student affairs about the habits of innovation and followed the keynote with a lunch to meet with some of the department heads. I remember turning on my hunter-gatherer lens and listening carefully to their frustrations with innovation. I knew that educators also shared the frustrations they were having across the country. I wanted to create some way that would allow me to connect with more educators, and not just the ones I get the chance to meet at a speaking engagement. I decided I would create an online course, and I knew I didn't want it to be like every other course with one lecturer giving a series of 10-minute video lectures on a topic. I started to rally the troops, and identified people that I knew could give guest lectures. When I realized I didn't have a short list of folks in K-12 that could guest lecture (but I knew by not including them I was missing a huge population of innovators), I improvised. I reached out to two organizations with a big contingency of teachers and pitched the opportunity to have them featured as guest lecturers. I worked with some friends to identify authors that might do some live Q&A sessions. While it took a while to figure the best way to explain my concept and my goals, when I figured that piece out, I found that each person was excited to help and participate.

Pioneers start from scratch. They are scrappy and look for every opportunity to lay new ground, as they go where no one has been before they improvise. In my experience, I couldn't find anyone that created a class curating so much outside content, so I had to create my pitch emails and craft my conversations with potential guest lecturers from scratch. There was a lot of improvising on the fly. As a pioneer trying to lay down a new framework, I had to work relentlessly for a good three to four weeks. I knew there would be a window to capture the attention of folks right when the school year ended before they took vacation, and I had to do everything I could to meet that projected launch date. I was filming lectures on weekends, sending out emails before the workday started and taking calls with folks when they got out of work. At the end of my first rookie year, it feels great to have over 50 enrolled including educators from across the country and even some from Australia!

After Courtney's first trip up to Boston and first few days on the job, she thought Erik was silly to hire her. Surely, there had to be someone with more experience in generating new leads or navigating the publishing process. Two years later, she now realizes that he wasn't mistaken. The one theme he could pull from looking at her experience was that she was a perpetual rookie. Each year of her professional career was spent doing a job no one had done the year before her. He didn't want someone that thought they knew everything there was to know about business development and publishing. He wanted someone that was up for the challenge of navigating new frontiers — someone that could create new models and not just follow the formula that lead to current models. If you feel like you're in a role for which you are completely unqualified, think again. Put on your rookie hat, and go for it.

I interviewed many different people for this book. People of all ages with various passions and talents told me their stories of how they found their niche. When I met Chloe Alpert, something was different. Here was a young woman, 22 years old, with more tenacity and grit than I had ever seen in someone before. She was like a superhero with absolutely no fear and incredibly determined to reach her wildest and most ambitious goals. Her story inspires any young person reading this book to go after their dreams with a wooden bat.

Chloe has always been ahead of her time. She started her first business when she was 12. She dual enrolled in college (Pennsylvania State University) and high school before she was 18. While attending high school and college *at the same time,* she taught professors how to use Adobe Creative Suite for digital purposes rather than the traditional method: print. Chloe studied abroad in England, searching for new opportunities and testing her potential. Teachers constantly told her to forget about digital design and continue doing things the old school way. But Chloe had bigger plans, and knew that technology and everything digital would be the wave of the future.

After receiving a degree in Gemology and Design and Communications, the young graduate knew that she had to create her own company. Here's Chloe describing how she felt after getting her diploma:

"I'm never going to be at my best working for someone else. I can't work for someone. I can work with someone...I can work with my equals and I can have people work for me. But, just knowing me personally, I will never be at my best...I will never be able to achieve the successes I want [by working for someone]."

Chloe saw that many areas were "right for disruption," but no one was capitalizing on them. She decided she wanted to start Teaman & Company, a colored gemstone company that considers itself "the jeweler of the millennial generation."

In 2012, Chloe began laying the foundation for her company. She wrote a 50-page business plan and executive summary. She began asking her mother about tradeshows. She started making business cards and buying domain names. Thinking that she needed work experience, Chloe also interned and worked for a couple San Francisco-based startups, mainly in the e-commerce sector. However, she foresaw problems with communication and structure that no one else seemed to notice. She became frustrated that no one seemed to take her suggestions seriously.

Deciding to dive head first into Teaman & Company, she won $100,000 in funding from 500 Startups and won first place in the Products and Services section at Berkeley Launch Competition.

Chloe has had many successes as she's navigated the world of business, finance, design and communications. It should come as no surprise, then, that she has strong opinions about millennials following their passion and conforming into traditional work structure.

Employees at Teaman & Company don't follow the typical structure of the 9 to 5 workday. Everyone typically arrive in the office between 10 to 10:30. If they need to leave at 3pm to go to a doctors' appointment, no one gets upset. What's most important, Chloe says, is that employees hit their daily and weekly goals. It doesn't matter if someone needs to go home and take a nap in the middle of the workday. As long as employees are productive and motivated to hit their targets, they decide the structure of their day.

Because everyone may not be in the same place at the same

time, communication and self-discipline is key, Chloe says. It's important that everyone communicates with their team. The results-driven atmosphere at Teaman & Company gives employees a sense of freedom and ownership over their projects.

However, Chloe isn't into bucking the system for the sake of being troublesome. She believes that while millennials may not fit into the business structure that has been in place for decades, they should be strategic about the way they spend their time. For example, she says that ambitious Gen Yers should be "making moves now, when you're 22, that will impact what you're doing when you're 30." Time shouldn't be wasted on jobs that aren't fulfilling or won't give you the experience you need for your next step.

Like a lot of the other people profiled in the book, Chloe has found that networking has helped the success of her business. People should curate their LinkedIn profiles to gain connections with people they may not be able to reach otherwise. LinkedIn has helped Chloe get in touch with investors and industry leaders to raise funding for Teaman & Company and raise awareness about the brand. "A warm intro is better than a cold one," Chloe says.

Having a general digital footprint is immensely important in today's day and age. Not knowing how to do something, like code or use Adobe Suite, is no longer an excuse for not being successful. Everything is searchable and can be learned by spending a week online. Chloe bases her hiring decisions off of how put-together her prospective employee's online presence is. She gave the scenario of two identical applicants applying for the same job with Teaman & Company. If one of them has an active Twitter account or personal website and the other one doesn't, she will always go with the one who has a digital footprint. As we all know, the Internet has shaped Generation Y. It's important that millennials leave their mark on the Internet, too.

The most important tip Chloe would give to fellow millennials is to take risks. "No one's going to hand you anything," she says, "you are just as able as anyone else in the world to be successful. Use what you've got and make it happen." Risk taking is easier now because most millennials don't have children, mortgages or other obligations. She's found that it's extremely important to start today rather than waiting for someone to give you a hand out.

Chloe Alpert is an entrepreneur who has immense experience to support the claims she's made about the future of business. I'd expect Chloe's drive, ambition and recognition to get stronger as her personal and gemstone brand grow and expand.

Reading about risk takers like Courtney and Chloe can be inspiring and also a little intimidating. Not everyone is wired this way. Many of us fear the unknown and struggle with "analysis paralysis," that phase we go through where we overthink ourselves out of the leap of faith. This is completely normal and happens to the majority of people, including me. However, since risk-taking is a big part of finding your niche, we wanted to include some tips. The next time you're facing a new situation or taking a big risk, try the following strategies written by Amanda Sol Peralta of Live In The Grey and adopted from the book *The Charisma Myth*:

1. De-stigmatize Discomfort

Risk makes us uncomfortable because we feel like we aren't in control. One way to overcome this feeling is to remind yourself of how completely normal it is to feel discomfort in this situation. For example, think of someone you greatly admire, someone who has accomplished amazing things. Imagine them in a similar situation, feeling equally scared and uncomfortable. (They all really have felt like that, by the way.) Now, think of all the other people in the world who are probably feeling the same way at this exact moment. You aren't crazy. You aren't overreacting. You're just human like everyone else, and you're trying to wrap your head around a new situation.

2. Neutralize Negativity

In these situations, we're often our own worst enemy. We see things from the worst possible angle, and before even giving ourselves a fair shot, we convince ourselves that things are going poorly. Instead, realize that your thoughts and perceptions aren't necessarily the objective truth. Try assigning a label to your feelings, like "self criticism" or "frustration." Think about them through the lens of a scientist. Your negative thoughts may simply be your brain's instinctive reaction to a high-stakes situation. Now, imagine that all of these thoughts in your mind are just noise from a radio. *Slowly turn down the dial.*

3. Re-write Reality

Let's say something goes really wrong, whether it's because you took a risk or because you didn't. You're here now, so what can you do about it? All it takes to turn a stressful situation into a positive one is a change in your perspective. You've probably heard something like this before, so how do you actually translate this into reality?

Let's think through a real situation. Maybe you just received a negative performance review at work. Find a piece of paper and write down *all the possible ways* in which this situation could actually end up being good for you. Imagine how this might be the first step in a series of events that leads to a great ending. Maybe the performance review shines a light on a problem that you can now work through so you can become incredible at what you do. Or maybe you realize the way your company measures you simply doesn't mesh with who you want to become.[xi]

By deciding to interpret bad situations as first steps in a story with a happy ending, not only will you see the light at the end of the tunnel but you'll also be equipped with the perspective to turn the situation around.

New York Times Bestselling Author Madeline Sheehan said, "There will always be a reason why you meet people. Either you need them to change your life or you're the one who will change theirs." Since I started taking risks and pushing my comfort zone, I have found that this quote holds true. But the scope is even broader when you allow serendipity to come into play, opening up new opportunities for you to explore.

A perfect example of this all started on December 30, 2008 on top of a lighthouse in Hilton Head, South Carolina when I proposed to my girlfriend, now wife Courtney. When she said yes, we delved into the real fun: wedding planning. Next to marrying Courtney, little did I know that meeting our wedding photographers, Chris and Suzanne LoBue owners of CLB Photography, would be one of the highlights of our wedding — and then a catalyst to finding my niche a few years later.

I still remember vividly the first time we met Chris and Suzanne in their studio in the basement of their home in Red Bank, NJ. When we arrived for our appointment, we were greeted by their two young daughters. Chris and Suzanne had it all down to a science and organized a babysitter every time they had an appointment so they wouldn't be distracted from their clients. Even in their tiny space, they always somehow made it work.

Chris and Suzanne immediately connected with us as people before they even mentioned anything about pictures, prices or logistics. It felt as though we knew them for years and they genuinely wanted to know about us then our relationship so they could find the best way to capture one of the special moments in our lives.

CLB Photography has come a long way since 2008, while still keeping that personal touch that initially drew us to them. The duo has moved into their own storefront with full-time staff and a large studio on the second floor. Chris and Suzanne were not only our wedding photographers, but they became part of our circle. The two of them are exceptional at connecting with a variety of personalities, but most of all, they are creative and take risks. They had a vision and grew their business all while living out their passion every day.

When I asked Chris to conduct a training seminar for my student marketing team at Rutgers, he kept things simple and shared some very important advice: "Do whatever it takes to get the shot." This philosophy has stuck with me and several of my team members over the years. They taught me to trust my gut and to realize that I am in charge of my vision. In your life, you determine how to capture the moment, you determine the risks you take and you determine how far you will go in life — no one else has that privilege for you.

Sometimes we put our relationships into boxes. I could have easily placed the LoBue's into the "business relationship" or "wedding planning" box, paid for our photos and moved on. However, when I meet someone as talented and passionate about their work as Chris and Suzanne, I think both about how I can connect with them and how I can build upon our relationship.

Look at those in your life who have found their niche, figure out new and different ways you can continue to build those relationships and learn from them. This will ease the burden of pushing your comfort zone because it reminds us that if they can do it then we can do it.

The career development process — from job searching to dealing with colleagues to getting the next promotion — is not easy. We often go at it alone, and when we are alone, we are more prone to believing the negative thoughts that tell us we're not good enough. If you want to live the life you've been dreaming of, you need to be open to getting help. I've learned that whether it's help on a project or finding a good listener or meeting with a life coach, seeking help is not just okay, it's actually recommended.

Imagine what we could accomplish if we didn't listen to the negative voices inside our heads. You know, the part of the brain that just spouts out negative comments like, "you can't do it," "you'll never be good enough" or "you're bad at that."

I think you know what I'm talking about.

Until a few months ago, my subconscious often got the best of me. I grew up as a quiet child and let my parents tell people I was shy. Soon enough, I began to believe it myself. I used the word "shy" as a crutch to mask my inner voice telling me that what I had to say wasn't good enough, wouldn't resonate with the people around me and that people were going to judge me. I've had these experiences all too often, both in my childhood and in my adult life.

But today, I can say these questions have been put to rest for me. I no longer question myself, no longer allow that negativity to sneak into my thoughts and I no longer doubt my vision.

How did I get here? It wasn't a magical pill or a quick fix. It started with a conversation with my good friend from graduate school, Stacy Rinaldi Campesi. Stacy and I worked together at Centenary College, but the main thing we have in common is our passion for leadership. When I met Stacy, she had recently been hired as the Coordinator of First Year Programs. She was an excellent mentor to her students and created programs that were innovative and engaging for students. She has since held two more positions in the education field, but even still, continued to feel as if something critical was missing. She finally decided to push herself out of her comfort zone and began taking classes to become a professional life coach.

During a visit with Stacy and her husband Chris, the conversation turned to our careers. I mentioned The Niche

Movement and shared some recent notables, but still wasn't as thrilled as I should have been to be talking about it. That's when Stacy put on her life coach hat and unleashed her new skill set.

Before this conversation, I always had a limited view of my work with The Niche Movement. I doubted my ability to take it full-time, I doubted that I would succeed and I doubted that I would be able to make it as an entrepreneur.

Through Stacy's questions and insight, we started to identity my vision and my values. She helped me recognize that I needed to be in an environment where I could carry out my own vision. I realized that my values, like being flexible, honest, hardworking, authentic, autonomous and a leader, didn't match up with my current environment. More often than not, I didn't believe in myself or stick up for my vision.

Around this time, I also realized I was making a lot of assumptions. Those voices in my head would comment on an interaction with a friend or colleague and would lead me to assume the worst of the situation. These assumptions held me back from achieving my true potential. I can't tell you how great it feels to not let those assumptions control me anymore.

After that conversation, I had a refreshed outlook on my work and The Niche Movement. I felt a new motivation and drive like I have never experienced. I realized that there truly is no better time than now to chase your dream. Stacy has continued to encourage me and has helped me lay out a very detailed plan to achieve my own happiness. She has helped quiet my subconscious to the point where I no longer hear those voices.

Stacy taught me how to silence the negative voices and comments I was creating in my head. She taught me how to cope with these voices and feelings, and simultaneously, has unlocked great potential I never knew I had. I learned that it's okay to talk things out with people. We live in a culture that suggests you should feel shameful for expressing your feelings, especially if the emotions are negative or doubtful. The truth is, there is no shame in expressing those emotions. Getting out of that negative cloud is the way you are going to grow, and as we know, the only thing worse than a negative mindset is a stagnant one.

When we talk about risk taking, I have to take a moment to acknowledge fellow introverts that perhaps struggle with leaning into discomfort more than their extrovert peers. Introverts are not necessarily shy individuals; they essentially prefer more minimally stimulating environments[xii]. For instance, conferences and career fairs with lots of stimulation can drain the energy of introverts and will have the opposite effect on extroverts. Introverts are also highly introspective and reflective, which can help them in a one-on-one interview for a job. Because there are unique challenges that introverts face, we brought in one of our experts on the topic to provide tips for those introvert readers that are working to find their niche.

One of our Niche Movement contributors, Amma Marfo is passionate about determining how introversion affects professionals and the students she works with. She landed on this topic after working with an "Extreme E," or extrovert, during graduate school. The opposites attracted, and the pair became friends; however Amma enjoyed defining her own qualities against the Extreme E. Introverts and extroverts had different needs, studying habits and preferences in the work environment. She took her observations and ideas to different conferences and saw that people responded positively and ultimately decided to write a book, called *The I's Have It* which was released in January 2014.

As she works with students each day, Amma understands the plight of the post-graduation job search. She has a few tips for introverts looking to start their career, though these tips are useful for extroverts, too.

- **Give yourself permission to experience "the wrong fit":** Not every job will have all of the requirements you desire in your dream job. And not every position you hold will feel like the right match. Allow yourself to be okay with having a somewhat undesirable experience. Use this to determine the type of environment you *do* want to work in at your next job.

- **Try not to be tied down to a specific job or idea:** It sucks not to receive your "dream job" upon graduation, especially when you've carefully researched and prepared for it! Try to vary your job search so that you have a multiple options that you'd be satisfied with. In other words, don't put all your eggs in one basket!

- **Learn how to manage introversion:** It's difficult being an introvert in a world that rewards extroversion! To make things easier for yourself before a meeting, ask for an agenda in advance so you can prepare for it. Take time to collect yourself — this can mean anything from taking a water break during a stressful day at work or going to the bathroom during an interview.

- **Know how you like to work:** Offices with open floor plans may cause difficulties for introverts. Take advantage of opportunities to work from home, or try coming in to work early before others arrive to get a bit more done.

- **Pay close attention:** If you're in a conversation with someone of influence (like a possible boss or a connection that can help you land a job) and they mention something that's important to them (like a topic they've studied heavily), remember the information and bring it up the next time you speak to them.

- **Think before responding:** Writing thank you cards and follow up emails allow you to take some time to craft your response and don't put you on the spot.

- **Do your research beforehand:** Read articles about the company's industry before you go in for an interview. Look at the news surrounding the company to find out what's important to the people who work there.

- **Use social media:** Open a dialogue with people and companies you want to work for. They'll certainly remember you!

- **Become okay with being an "and":** College culture influences students to pick one interest and follow it for the rest of their lives; however, that's not exactly how today's culture works. You don't have to pick just one interest and focus on it forever. It's fine to have multiple interests. You can be a biology teacher *and* do poetry readings at night. Or become a veterinarian *and* a freelance writer.

Finding your niche can be a difficult process. But Amma is comfortable with that, saying, "My niche is helping other people find theirs." She revels in the process of helping introverts manage their personality types. And it's extremely rewarding when others are helped by her work and research!

I have talked to so many people that have bucket list items they want to achieve, ideas they want execute, businesses they want to start or blogs they want to create. And so often, I see them get caught up in figuring out the plan first, and then making the big move.

- You want to start a business? Talk with your boss about an agreed upon last day of work.
- You want to start blogging? Tell all your followers, friends, family when the launch date will be.
- You want to do fitness challenge of some sort that you are not prepared for (10K, mud run, etc.)? Find one, and sign up.
- You want to write a book? Announce a publishing date on your blog.
- You want to create something you don't have funds for? Sign up for a Kickstarter account and build your campaign.

The truth is, you can start a Kickstarter campaign, apply to TED, quit your job or sign up for a Tough Mudder without knowing all the details. However, by choosing to make the first move the biggest one, now you have some serious motivation to prepare and figure it out. This next story from Megan Schwab a Niche Movement contributing editor and Academic Advisor at Florida State University, is a great example of taking a leap of faith and learning to believe in yourself.

The Myth of the Stage

Written by Megan Schwab

When I got accepted to present my ideas at TEDxFSU this year, I was thrilled! My first thought was "oh my gosh they like my idea!" followed quickly by the terrifying, earth shattering doubt, "They're going to find out I'm a fake!"

Why was this the first (well, almost first) thought to pop into my brain when something good happened?

I call it the Myth of the Stage, and it's a big part of why we accept far less for our selves than we truly deserve.

So here is the Myth: The person on stage is right. The person on stage knows what they are talking about, and their ideas are valid.

Maybe this myth comes from our early days in a traditional classroom setting, listening to an all-knowing teacher. Maybe it comes from watching movies and documentaries. Wherever it comes from, you know you feel it in your mind. It's the same little part of you that says it's valid to pay over $100 to watch someone play an instrument onstage at Lincoln Center, when it's not worth giving a dollar to the man riffing on the guitar on a street corner. They both add music to our lives, right? But one is on a *stage*.

So this myth lives inside us, and it's part of what holds us back. If we are not on the stage, how do we know if we're valid? How do we know if we belong on stage? We can wait for someone to pick us. An employer, a casting director or a conference coordinator can decide you are worth something and put you out there for the world to see. You shouldn't leave it up to them, though!

Here are my three reasons it's important to find your stage and start singing:

1. The Stage is Everywhere

Now more than ever you have the chance to set up your soapbox, climb on up and spread your message! You no longer have to wait for an editor to publish your ideas — just start a blog. You don't have to wait for a T.V. station to broadcast your idea — make your own video. In the age of the Internet, it is easier than ever before to connect with an audience. They might not all love you (there are trolls under every bridge, of course), but the more you share, the more you will find people who connect with what you are saying.

2. Most People Won't Bet on an Unknown

There are those risk-takers out there who thrive on the thrill of something new and unknown, but in general, the people making the decisions about who gets hired, who gets on the stage and who gets in front of the camera got their jobs by consistently choosing correctly. Now, in a time where there are more people to hire than ever, these "pickers" are under a lot of pressure to make the right choice.

Knowing you already have an audience you've connected with makes it easier for them to bet on you. If you're a band just starting out, booking agents want to know how many tickets you can sell. The same applies now for hiring agents, editors and everything else. So just start doing what you do, build up a loyal base and then you can get "picked" if you still want to.

3. Your Message Matters

If you have an idea, a passion or a creation to share that seems totally out of the blue, chances are it's even more important than you think. It's hard to be the first one to try something new. You could fail, and you could end up looking stupid. But if it's something truly new, why would you want to hide it away? Can you imagine where we would be if Thomas Edison decided that an electric light was too risky? Or that people wouldn't be interested? Inspiration comes for a reason, and by keeping your idea to yourself, you're depriving the world of something that could be truly, truly awesome.

There are many more reasons than this to share your message, but next time you doubt yourself, remember:

The Myth of the Stage is just that: A myth.

Chapter 4

Skip Your Career Fair

We are experiencing a significant disconnect between a college degree and a full-time, well paying job. The latest study found that one in eight recent college graduates is unemployed, and half of those employed hold jobs that do not require a college degree.[xiii] There are many factors to blame for this lack of return on investment in a college education, but some presume that these stats are a reflection of a career development field that is ripe for disruption.[xiv] In *Rethinking Success: From the Liberal Arts to a Career in the 21st Century*, co-author Andy Chan states, "While transformational changes have occurred in the world of work, many college career offices look and function the same way they did twenty years ago."[xv] I couldn't agree more. The career fair was an approach designed decades before digital technology existed and long before over a third of the U.S. workforce was made up of freelancers and entrepreneurs.

I won't say that a career fair will never lead to a job post-graduation, but I will say that I have yet to meet someone that has found a job through a career fair. Young people are finding jobs in very different ways than they did 20 or more years ago. According to a recent study, many young people are leveraging digital tools to enter the job search process. Below are a few of the key findings from the study:

- Nearly 60% of young people said that a search engine was the first place they went to look for jobs
- 80% of 18 – 24 year olds said they have used social media to look for jobs

- 1 in 6 said they would visit social media first when searching for employment opportunities.
- Twitter was the most popular form of social media for this purpose.[xvi]

This chapter will provide a variety of innovative approaches to the job search and career development process. It is also designed to help young people that are utilizing modern job search techniques, but are struggling to navigate different types of search tools as well as interpreting whether a job is a good fit for them. We want to share some tactics and things you can do to avoid a crowded gym or student center with a hundred of employers who are probably there for the free lunch and day out of the office.

Let's face it — most companies are at career fairs because their competitors are. They also set up a table because no one ever told them to seek talent elsewhere. But let's be real: resume, after resume, after resume gets piled on their table and put into their car when they leave. It's a shame, as companies pay sometimes more than $500-$600 just for a table to talk to hundreds, if not thousands of college students so desperately looking for a job.

But student leaders, you shouldn't be desperate. You worked hard while in college, you got involved, you built your leadership skills and are crossing off some pretty amazing things on your "before I grow up list." What I want to tell you is: don't be one of the hundreds or thousands at your next career fair. Depending on what you want to do, here is our first suggestion:

You want to look for intimate settings that aren't crowded with other college students.

Here is one:

Creative Mornings takes place once a month in over 40 cities worldwide (listen up to all of you studying abroad). Even if you live within a 90-minute commute to one of these cities, it is worth it. Every month, they have a theme — anywhere from design to marketing to money. Then, their chapter organizes and finds a well-known or up-and-coming figurehead that has found their niche.

The best part is they provide breakfast, it's free and they host them at some unique places. When I went in July to NYC, I heard Kellie Anderson talk about design and I got to network with more than 100 artists, graphic designers, programmers and even the founder SwissMiss. Oh yeah, and it was held in one of the most creative offices I've ever seen, called the X/O group, who started The Knot, The Bump and The Nest.

However, I noticed that there were no college students. If I am a college student interested in getting into design, photography, videography, web design, marketing, event planning and the like, I would be incredibly excited. Here's the thing: unless you are digging deep, scouring Twitter and networking extensively, you will never hear about opportunities like this.

Now, getting a ticket for a Creative Morning meetups is not easy, as they are free and go quickly on the Monday they are released, so you need to act fast. However, most hosts are very accessible — when I emailed them to try to get two more tickets, they at least gave me a response (from a real human).

Here's our advice if you get shut out: hunt down the organizer and contact them. If you have a skill such as videography or photography, they are always looking for help to document their events. If you have your own blog or doing an assignment for a course, use that as an excuse to get in; depending on the person you contact, they may have a soft spot to let you in. As a last ditch effort, you could just show up and explain you are a student. Worst-case scenario: you don't get in and you go explore the town or stumble upon some other company.

The job search is a lonely process. If you think about it, 99 percent of the time you are by yourself (generally late at night, if we're being honest), scrolling through job postings, one after another. Then, when you do stumble upon a posting you love and are qualified for, you spend more time and energy crafting the perfect cover letter, updating your resume, and more often than not, filling out an application to submit to an applicant tracking system.

The cycle goes on and on, and when you finally reintroduce yourself back into society the next day, your friends and family ask you, "Hey, how's the job search going?" This repetitive cycle wears even the most ambitious job seeker down, and all of a sudden, the talented professional will start to second-guess their skills, potential, and calling in life.

Before you get to this point — or even hit send on your next job application — take a few steps back and ask yourselves these three questions:

1. What are three things you would do for free?

I like to pose these questions with everyone I start to work with, both one-on-one and during speaking engagements. This is a powerful question and requires a lot of thought, but once you begin to identify a few things you love so much that you would do them without compensation, you're truly onto something. Once you are able to answer the question, you can begin to drill down into specific industries, companies, positions to focus on in your job search. A common cliché is find three hobbies: one that will make you money, one that will keep you in shape (or sane) and one where you can be creative.

Here, I also recommend that if you can't find the job you're most passionate about, create it yourself. We live in a world of limitless connection and virtually unlimited resources at your fingertips (many shared in this book) that can turn a passion project into a business in no time. Just note, it requires a ton of hustle, self-esteem and perseverance.

2. What do people around you say you are really good at?

I love this question and believe that everyone should continually ask this question starting early on in their career. A matter of fact I would challenge you to start asking this question in your junior or senior year of college. Any chance you have, ask your professors, supervisors, advisors, best friends and family, "What do you think are my strengths?" or "What are my strongest skills?" Their answers will give you insight into where your interests and skill sets align.

3. What is something you have done in the last 6-12 months that made you feel invincible?

A student of mine shared this question with me during our six-week Niche Discovery cohort we ran in spring of 2013, and I have asked myself this question just about once a month since. It's from Scott Dinsmore's Live Your Legend site, and it is so powerful.

When you find that thing that makes you feel invincible, you will stop at nothing to achieve it. If you are applying (or already working for) a job at a company or in an industry you are not passionate about, you are not going to have a "do whatever it takes" mentality.

The more time and thought you put into those questions, the better your outcome will be. Ask yourself these questions, and ask them often. Make sure your values, skills and goals are still lining up.

Many people that feel stuck in their career ponder the idea of going back to school. Some will look for a program that will teach them a specific skill set, like those that go back to learn coding or computer programming. Many often contemplate the idea of graduate school. Recent data shows that the unemployment rate for those with a master's degree is around 3.4%, compared to 4% for people with a bachelor's degree, and the median annual earning is about $12,000 more per year for those with a master's degree versus bachelors. However, it's important to note the payoff varies.[xvii]

The important piece to remember is that graduate school should never be something you pursue without thought or intention. I see many students pursue graduate degrees because they felt that it was the only choice or as a way to avoid the job search. Unfortunately, many of these individuals never finished the program and were left with substantial bills to pay for the classes they did take. It's not always a bad decision. I have my master's in leadership and feel as though the coursework and experiences better prepared me for my unique career path. The point is to give it some thought and know that it is not for everyone, as you are about to find out in this next story about one of The Niche Movement's contributors.

Over and over again, Nicole Booz finds herself returning to the idea of continuing her education with a graduate degree. Over and over again, she finds herself deciding not to.

Nicole's undergraduate degree is a Bachelor of Science in Psychology with a minor in Human Development. Building a career in either of these fields requires more schooling. Why would she choose them as her area of study without committing herself to seeing it through?

She chose psychology because, for her, it has always been psychology that drew her interest. She had the privilege of holding a human brain during her AP Psychology class her senior year of high school and that pretty much sealed the deal; nothing else really compared to that experience. Human behavior is one of the most fascinating things she has ever encountered and quite frankly, she couldn't see herself studying anything else.

Throughout her undergraduate career, she toyed with adding another major or minor, and even got her feet wet a few times. She considered finding another less-committal, more-marketable major. She took a few different classes, but nothing else could hold her attention like a psychology course. Her favorite psychology course she ever took was Psychology of Organizational Processes. Unfortunately, she wasn't able to take it until her senior year — not that it mattered much anyway, as it was the only Industrial/Organizational course offered at her institution.

Upon graduation, she made the decision to take a six-month break (which she highly recommends to everyone). After a hectic and less than enjoyable senior year, she desperately needed time to get back in touch with the part of her that wanted to learn for fun and that enjoyed the process rather than the part of her that sought to check the requirements off of her four-year plan. She needed to take time for herself to understand her values and to understand where she wanted to be career-wise five and ten years from now.

As you can imagine, this is where grad school comes into play. To make use of her psychology degree, whether as a school counselor or a social worker (her two preferred paths), she would need to attend grad school. She spent time over the next few months looking into programs both near and far, making phone calls and gathering information. But in the end, instead of committing, she deferred.

She couldn't see herself sitting through more lectures or spending hours and hours in small groups discussing nuances of a particular subject. That kind of learning no long appealed to her. As it turns out, she decided the world is her classroom.

Following her six-month break (which stretched until the end of 2012), she officially decided grad school wasn't for her, at least not at this point in her life. So she started a business instead.

After Nicole's husband got a job in Seattle and the couple moved cross-country, she decided to take some time off to get adjusted to all of the changes happening in her life.

She'd also always wanted to start a blog, and after contributing to a few online publications, Nicole decided to branch out on her own.

GenTwenty, launched in the spring of 2013, became a platform for young women to share their stories, and ultimately advice, with others. Nicole enjoyed reading other people's stories online, rather than always simply reading editorial pieces, and wanted to bring that same sense of community and comradery to her own blog. The brand has evolved over time; Nicole likes to keep her readers in mind when determining the mission and direction of the blog.

Currently, the team at GenTwenty is working to remove the stigma around not knowing the direction your life is headed in. People look down upon others who don't have a specific answer to the questions "So, what are you doing now?" "What projects are you working on?" and "Where do you see yourself in 10 years?" The team is focusing on sharing more stories about how women figured out what was next for them.

Nicole's main piece of advice to college students is to not stress out. She understands the pressure that comes with a looming graduation, anxious parents and strident college administrators. And while people continuously refer to "your first job out of college," Nicole says, many students fail to realize that your college career is part of your first career. Take advantage of many opportunities so you can have a grasp on the things that you do and do not like.

That being said, the path to success is littered with both successes and failures, and both should be taken in stride. Trial and error is the only way to figure out whether a certain field is one that you'd like to pursue. Making sure that something feels right is also a great way to gauge whether a job or particular field would be a good fit for you.

She also suggests that students sign up for classes that interest them, rather than simply finding classes that align with their major. For example, Nicole had always wanted to take a creative writing class while she attended the University of Maryland, but it definitely didn't fit in to her psychology major scheme. Doing so might have changed the course of her college career, and Nicole might have winded up doing something completely different from what she was used to. Extending yourself out of your comfort zone can strengthen (and sometimes challenge) the beliefs you hold.

A final tip is that students should focus on networking. Although people often feel awkward about talking to someone they've never met, its an integral part of success. Develop a 30-second elevator speech about your goals and where you're headed. Send emails and try cold calling. Most importantly, learn how to connect with people and make yourself memorable to them.

By remaining true to herself and authentic to her goals, values and brand, Nicole Booz has built a platform that provides advice and information to 20-something women. GenTwenty continues to be a space for women to share their stories, aspirations and dreams. Look out for more milestones from Nicole's team in the future.

When it comes to young people doing what they love, society often sends mixed messages. On one hand, we have our commencement speakers and graduation cards filled with inspirational message telling you to go after your dreams. But when the graduation party is over and the diplomas have come in the mail, reality sets in, and those same people tell you to do whatever you can to just get any job you can.

They are probably trying to be helpful by nudging you to the first employer that offers you a paycheck and some semblance of job security. This is a problem. As a young person, you are in the best possible environment and circumstances (most of the time) to take risks, big risks!

Someone I know who has always lived life to the fullest and is living proof that taking risks can end positively is my friend Nina Duong.

Nina grew up in Texas and when it came time for her to go to college, she enlisted in the Army as a means to pay for her education. Her college experience included all the great times in and out of the classroom, just like yours did, but it also included a tour of duty in Iraq. When she returned from her deployment, Nina took on a position in the residence life department at her alma mater, University of North Texas. She loved her experience as a student leader and had incredible mentors in the field that lead her to pursue Student Affairs as a career. This set up for Nina's first (of many) leaps of faith.

She was in the process of applying to graduate schools and needs to submit a list of schools that she wanted to send her GRE scores to. She had one open spot on her list, and after receiving three different calls from students and family from New Jersey, she took the calls as a sign and added Rutgers University to the list as a final choice to round out her list.

When it came time for interviews, it was no other than my wife Courtney who interviewed Nina for a graduate position. The position was brand new, so Nina took yet another leap of faith and accepted the position based on the interview and vision Courtney was painting for her.

When she first arrived to Rutgers, Courtney somehow convinced Nina to play on the softball team. I still remember the first game, before Nina arrived to the field. Courtney was telling us, "I invited my new graduate student to play. She says she is terrible at softball, but she is an Iraqi war veteran, so how bad could she possibly be at softball?"

Turns out, Nina was awful at softball, but she brought the same excitement and enthusiasm that she brought with her to Rutgers to the field. She came to every game and always gave it her all. When our team made it to the championship, she gave her teammates one of the best pep talks I've ever heard in my life.

Nina's story is a testament to the leap of faith. She could have easily said, "Why would I apply to Rutgers? I know nothing about it, and have no connection to that school." or "Why would I take a position with a brand new program when I have the opportunity to take a position at a long-standing program?" or even "Why would I play softball when I'm terrible at it?" But Nina doesn't second-guess a thing; she just goes for it. She pushes her comfort zone constantly — sometimes too much.

In Nina's story, the most daring leap of faith came after she graduated from her master's program. She had one of the best resumes of any grad looking for a job that year; she easily had her choice between nearly any institution she wanted. But Nina had a different idea, and she wanted to chase her new dream.

One night while she was out with friends, Nina came up with an ingenious idea for packaging cosmetics. With the entrepreneurial spirit burning within her, Nina knew if she was going to make it happen, now was the time. She took some money she earned from her service in the war and traveled the world. She knew these experiences would allow her to clear her head and prepare her for this new entrepreneurial endeavor. She thought, "When else will I have the opportunity to travel like this?" When she came home, she got right to work. She currently works part-time for Apple, but spends the rest of her time working on her new business.

At the end of the day, Nina can always dust off her student affairs resume. There are folks out there who would love to have Nina join their team if she is ever ready to pursue a career in higher education. But Nina is young and she is using her 20s to travel, learn more about herself and the world and to take the plunge on a bright idea.

Nina has taught me to trust my gut. She deeply believes that everything happens for a reason. She has taught me to find the silver lining in my experiences and to take more risks. She serves as a shining example to young professionals that need to hear that it's okay to take risks, to take a break, to follow an interest or to pursue a passion. The ride may be a little bumpy and may take some unexpected twists and turns that you don't anticipate, but if you are a good person and continue to work hard, you will come out just fine.

Remember, you are only young once in your life. When you have a mortgage and a family and bills to pay, it becomes significantly harder to take risks. Go for a job that fulfills you and not just your bank account. You will gain incredible insights, perspective and experiences from the risks you take in your 20s.

Remember, it is sometimes more dangerous to be cautious. Maybe your first step is volunteering or working abroad. Look for a variety of different opportunities — not just the ones on your university's career search site. Not all career paths look alike, and not all definitions of success are the same. Trust your gut and know that success is not always found by following the pack.

After interviewing many individuals that have found employment happiness, I have come to realize that one's career can and will change many times throughout their lifetime. This is a more modern concept that disrupts most traditional career development constructs. Even more, our job market is changing now more than ever. Sixty-five percent of all grade school students will work in jobs that have not been invented yet.[xviii] Finding your niche means having some flexibility and being able to adapt to our own circumstances as well as the current job market. No one knows this better than Alena Gerst. She refers to this as finding "boutique careers" and her story brings this concept to life.

Alena found her niche as a mind-body wellness coach and works as a psychotherapist and yoga teacher in New York City. She combined her passion for helping people with her skills in psychology and yoga to create a holistic therapy practice. In addition to working at various NYC-area hospitals, Alena uses yoga to rehabilitate people suffering from injuries. Though Alena works face-to-face with many different types of people each day, her job wasn't always socially oriented.

In college, Alena believed she was going to become a lawyer. Upon graduating from Northern Arizona University, she moved to New York and became a dancer and performer. She worked diligently, and ultimately continued in the performing arts for 10 years until her life changed when she became sick and had to stop dancing. Although she followed traditional medical practices, Alena felt that her condition improved greatly with the addition of more holistic methods, such as yoga and psychotherapy. After recovery, Alena felt that others could benefit from using holistic medicine while being rehabilitated.

Once recovered, Alena decided to get her Masters in Social Work and a yoga teaching certification. Through her life experiences in her 20s and early 30s, Alena's passion finally started to shine through.

Alena understands something that many millennials may not realize: working a 9 to 5 job is simply not for everyone. The lack of interest in a typical 9 to 5 is nothing to be ashamed of; however, it is important to realize that these typical careers are not for you.

Rather, Alena puts emphasis on "boutique careers," or jobs that are created by combining many different (and sometimes contradictory) interests into one career. Alena created her own boutique career by incorporating all of her unique skill sets into one profession. One way to launch your boutique career is by networking.

Alena says that all of her positions at hospitals and information about different careers have been gained by simply talking to people. The more you speak to people, the more you "plant seeds"; although you may not have your dream job at the moment, you're laying the foundation for future success and career happiness.

A final note that Alena makes is that a person should always be content with their chosen career — at least in that moment until they can make a change. Unhappiness in the workplace can lead to increased stress (which, as a psychotherapist and because of her past experiences, Alena knows a lot about). Even if you can't have your dream job right out of school, you should always be doing something that makes you want to get out of bed in the morning. Happiness on the job leads to a healthier, more satisfied you.

The best advice Alena can leave is this: "Whatever it is you want to do, just give yourself permission and start."

Much like a shotgun start to a race, your career can give you an adrenalin rush. Embrace that feeling, and trust that your support network around you will be there to pick you up if you fall. This next story is about a couple that found their niche — quite literally — running towards their passion. My friend Laura Chegwidden Jacobs, a close friend of mine from high school, and her husband Joe Jacobs, have taken something they love and turned it into a career path.

In high school, Laura was a star athlete who played field hockey, basketball and track. Running seems to be part of her DNA; all of her siblings are also athletes. Joe also has running in his blood. He ran in college and has since worked for several running companies, including Mizuno. This is just one of the reasons Laura and Joe are perfect for each other. Running is their lifestyle, it's their passion, it's their calling. They even named their first child Miles.

When you do something you love, success follows. After Laura played field hockey in college, she became a Physical Education teacher and eventually got into coaching cross-country, basketball and track. Despite all the activity, for Laura, it never feels like work. She went on to be named North Jersey's Cross Country Coach of the Year in 2011 and continues to organize fundraising races for education.

Laura and Joe took their love for running even further and went all-in and opened a Sneaker Factory location in Florham Park, NJ. Opening up a brand new store and going into business for yourself is a huge risk, but not for Laura and Joe. The two have succeeded because of their work ethic, their support system and their passion for running.

What Joe and Laura have taught me is that with the right values, you really can have it all. They found their niche and turned it into their lifestyle. They are succeeding at what they love, both individually and as husband and wife. They look something simple, something that has guided both of their lives, and turned it into a career path.

I have never once heard them complain about their choices or the heavy workload. Going all-in on your niche comes with risks, but if you fully commit to living your passion, success will come to you.

Many people find themselves in a conflict between passion and paycheck. Laura and Joe have worked very hard to make both passions a priority while paying the bills. This isn't always feasible. In addition, there are times in your career where you may find yourself in a crossroads concerning your loyalty to social issues and your desire for a more comfortable lifestyle. A bigger paycheck might not just be an option for some; circumstances like the illness of a loved one or the loss of one's savings can put serious pressure on an individual to find a high paying job. Everyone's circumstances are different and all are valid reasons for considering a more lucrative career. In this next story, you'll see how social enterprises are striking a balance between purpose driven work and a well paying job.

Laura Zax has been an agent of social change since she began kindergarten. Growing up in the Washington, D.C. area, Laura attended Georgetown Day School, one of the first integrated academic in the country. Later, she worked at Ashoka, a distinguished international nonprofit. Upon deciding to switch jobs after a few years at Ashoka, Laura knew she wanted to continue to make an impact in her community.

Enter Harry's, a startup that sells razors and other facial products to men directly online. Laura joined the company a month before their launch and become the Manager of Social Innovation. A fundamental aspect of the company's business model and philosophy is that companies should leverage their core business for social good. Harry's asset is the multitude of "21st century skill sets" available in the office.

Using their business savvy, the founders developed a community engagement model called "Harry's 1 + 1." One percent of company sales and one percent of company time are donated to organizations in the nonprofit sector that prepare people who are entering the workforce. This particular mission resonates heavily with the team at Harry's. Razors are a symbol of growing up, getting ready for work and looking your best. The company thought it was best to assist those institutions that work with people searching for a career.

Harry's has also created H'University, a program that helps college-aged individuals cultivate the skills they need to land their first job. Participants watch six webinars with people from the real world of startups and business development, such as Neil Blumenthal of Warby Parker and David Chang of Momofuku. These webinars are meant to inspire students and provide role models for them to look up to. H'University also connects participants with hiring partners for internships at 21st century workplaces like Sweetgreen and Blue Apron.

Laura is a big advocate for startups and the range of skills that can be learned working at one. Her suggestion for finding post graduation advice is, admittedly, not exactly traditional. She believes that recent grads should manage their expectations and realize that they still have time to figure out what they want to do. She dismisses the idea that because students graduate college they're all of a sudden supposed to know what they want to do.

Laura acknowledges that it takes time to figure that out, saying, "You're a freshman at life when you graduate. Listen to yourself and notice what pieces of each experience were good, and which were bad. Then use that 'data' to inform your decision making as you choose your next role." She also thinks that students should expose themselves to as many different types of people as possible. When at an interview or receiving a tour of the office, think, "Are these people I would want to be hanging out with?" You'll be spending a lot of time with your coworkers, so you want to be sure you'll enjoy their company.

Her advice for college students trying to stick out from under the sea of resumes is simple: start something. She's found that if an applicant is passionate about something, it will become evident in their resume. If you like web design, for example, start a blog about web design. Hiring managers want to know about your interests and that you're a go-getter. She also believes that the "other skills" section of your resume is a great place to show what you're really like. The HR team at Harry's loves to read resumes with a bit of flavor: for example, writing "Understanding of basic Spanish (and taco expert)." Companies want to know who you are outside of the office!

Since becoming a manager at Harry's over a year ago, Laura Zax has been able to fulfill her dream of advancing social change. As more and more businesses are taking note of

Harry's success and the social-good company model, the company continues to grow and consider new ways to be a leader in innovation and community service.

Chances are, you won't find Harry's at a career fair this fall. Companies like Harry's are counting on their current employees to recruit other capable and talented friends. They will also have a heavy online presence, so searching sites like Idealist.org or GlassDoor.com is a great place to start looking for jobs like Laura's.

Another unique path that is often missing from any traditional career development programs or messages to grads and students is the rapidly growing field of solopreneurs. Erica Swallow illustrates why this movement is growing at warped speed in her post, *A Field Guide to Solo Entrepreneurship*, "Web languages and technologies are more accessible than ever, with tutorials, classes and resources just clicks away. Fundraising has been democratized, with sites like Kickstarter and Indiegogo enabling users to validate demand for their products easily, all while pulling in dough to get started. And co-working spaces, hackathons, incubators, accelerators and business competitions are all the rage, offering would-be entrepreneurs bounds of opportunities to get started."[xix]

In this next story, we learn about Kali Hawlk's journey to solopreneurship. Much like thousands of graduates, she faced the struggle of finding a job with a very focused and traditional major. How she took matters into her own hands is an inspiring story that illustrates the creative new options all graduates have at their fingertips, even if their career services office never mentioned these alternatives.

Kali Hawlk always knew she wanted to write.

But the only career options given to history majors at her university were for them to continue their education and become a professor. Her school's career center focused on business and finance majors; those who were supposed to be guiding Kali through her final years of college did not provide much help in her career search.

After graduating in 2011, Kali began searching for writing jobs in Atlanta, Georgia. She looked for three months after graduating, constantly sending resumes but never hearing a response from the companies she truly wanted to work for. Many of Kali's peers were in the same situation, searching for positions but not being hearing back from hiring managers and HR departments. To make matters worse, Atlanta is a business-focused city — there simply weren't many opportunities available for people who wanted to create content.

Kali finally landed a job doing data entry for a firm. Though it was completely unrelated to anything she wanted to do, Kali finally had a source of income. After completing a grant-writing course soon after finding the data entry job, Kali reaffirmed the idea that she wanted to write for a living. Kali would finish her data entry work in about 4 hours, leaving her four more hours to work on her other personal projects. During her free time at the office, Kali began to craft her side hustle, which ultimately became her acclaimed blog *Common Sense Millennial.*

Millennials enjoy flexible work environments, Kali says. Typical 9 to 5s are not necessarily the most productive hours for certain people to work. Some people work better during the early morning hours, while others prefer to wake up late and do their jobs late into the night. The best companies to work for are those that understand and embrace this flexibility.

Gen Yers also need to have a sense of purpose in their role at work. It's important to know that you're being productive and making a difference in someone's life, no matter how small. People need to find your work useful.

Finally, it's imperative that companies embrace modern technology and new methods of completing old projects. Things don't have to be done a certain way simply because that's the way they've always been done. Businesses that are open to change and put a focus on employee happiness and office culture will always be successful.

A huge red flag to look out for when choosing companies to work for, Kali says, is whether you see "a sea of cubicles when you walk in" for your interview. She warns that these companies are not conducive to flexibility and being open to new ideas. It's important that companies constantly challenge the status quo and look to improve.

It's a great sign when you can tell that the office culture is not overly formal, and hiring managers recognize that you have a life outside your job. During an interview, be sure to gauge the degree of formality within the office setting. Ask questions like: "Is there any potential for flexibility in terms of employee schedules? Does everyone have to be at work at a specific time or is there an option for alternatives like telecommuting, or coming in an hour early and leaving an hour early?"

Kali's blog, Common Sense Millennial, helps young adults achieve financial security and stability by educating them about investing, saving and building a digital footprint. She started the blog for somewhat selfish reasons — she wanted to have an online portfolio of her writing, as her resume simply wasn't opening enough doors. By engaging in conversation, posing questions to fellow bloggers and sending emails, Kali grew her audience and became active in the personal finance blogosphere.

Though Common Sense Millennial initially began as an opportunity for Kali to share her writing, she began to branch out into content management and content marketing for financial planners. She launched the blog in November 2013, and by April 2014, Kali was making more money from her blogging and freelance work than she was making at her day job. Though she was eager to work for herself, she stuck it out at her day job for a few extra months before her workload became unbearable. Then she quit and focused on her online presence full time.

Whether you hate your day job, or have a great idea that you want to share with the world, Kali's advice is that young adults stick it out and continue working at their day job while building their project or escape on the side. The job, no matter how dreadful, allows you to provide for yourself financially. If you don't have the monetary means to care for yourself, there's no way you'll be able to grow your business.

She also suggests that people stop second-guessing themselves and "just go for it." Mistakes are positive because they keep you moving forward and give you an opportunity to learn and grow.

Networking is also extremely important to achieving career goals. "Get yourself out there and find someone you admire," Kali says. "Email them and ask how you can help. Look at how other people have done what you want to do." And when all else fails: "Google it!"

Having an "accountability buddy" to share your strengths, weaknesses, wins, losses and progress is also helpful. Simply surrounding yourself with positive people that believe in your goals and ambitions is a great motivator. Kali spoke to her parents, in-laws and husband, who all encouraged her to follow her dreams.

A final word of advice from Kali involves crafting a "grandma friendly" elevator speech. This will help you clearly and succinctly explain yourself and your ideas to people who may not be familiar with what you want to do. Put it in terms that even your grandmother could understand. A simple template could be something like, "I do/make _____ to help/achieve _____." For example, Kali's pitch sounds something like this, "I do content management for financial professionals. I've created a platform to teach 20-something's how to do more with their money." As the freelance economy grows, these types of speeches will be increasingly important.

After less than a year of blogging about finances to a millennial audience, Kali Hawlk was named one of US News and World Report's 37 Personal Finance Experts to Follow On Twitter. She was able to quit her monotonous day job and focus on building her personal brand full time. She's found that with hard work, dedication and a bit of networking, success within the blogosphere is possible, and even lucrative.

Sometimes your intuition will tell you when the next move is needed in your career before anyone else will notice. One in five individuals feel that fostering a comfortable and challenging work environment is key to keeping employees engaged.[xx] That gut feeling about engagement with your work can determine a lot. Disengaged employees are less productive, less healthy and will often undermine the work of engaged employees.[xxi] It's important to listen to your instincts and work on making changes in your career if you are feeling disengaged.

Meghan St. John took a leap of faith after feeling bored and uninterested at work, and the outcome has been exponentially better than she could have imagined.

Meghan is living every 20-something's dream. She's working in a creative environment where her suggestions, thoughts and feelings are noted and validated. She has control over the projects she works on, and works on many different tasks each day.

There's never a dull moment.

Meghan joined ZinePak, a publication targeted toward super fans of various celebrities, including Selena Gomez, Taylor

Swift and Luke Bryan, after working for UNICEF for three years. Although she felt like she was making a difference, Meghan eventually became bored. Her work got monotonous. She "wanted to get her hands dirty," something that wasn't happening at the non-profit. She initially didn't even know what a start-up was, let alone being familiar with start-up culture. These things were never discussed at Seton Hall University, where Meghan went for her undergraduate degree in PR and journalism, nor did her circle of friends ever breach the topic.

Though she had only been at ZinePak for two months at the time of her interview, the noticeable differences between the start-up and non-profit have Meghan completely sold on the benefits of the former. Her coworkers are all "equally as passionate" about the success of ZinePak, something that motivates Meghan to continue to crush goals and think about new ways to bring innovation to her duties. She also enjoys being able to work on various different projects in one day, and that her days are always different.

The relaxed company culture allows for a lot of direct contact with the company founders, Kim Kaupe and Brittany Hodak, and her direct superiors. Working for ZinePak, Meghan has also been able to strengthen different skills than those she was formally trained in. Having the ability to juggle multiple projects at one time is also a huge asset for being triumphant in today's job market. Organization is key when assuming different roles within a company. Hiring managers will also appreciate your ability to manage many projects and adhere to tight deadlines.

Once Meghan decided to switch careers, she began to send her resume to companies that she was interested in. But she never got a response. Finally, she says, "I realized I needed to start talking to people." She utilized her networks to find openings at different companies. Networking is also essential to learning about opportunities. Meghan says that simply telling everyone (from doctors to friends of friends to previous professors) "I'm looking for a job" reminds people to keep you in mind if they hear about an opening. This is a simple way to network that may be overlooked by recent grads.

Meghan's most important piece of advice to young professionals, college students and recent graduates is to take risks. She argues that because Generation Yers are young, they can bounce back from any failures that happen along the way. The lessons that are learned through failures will also inevitably help you make your next move. She also suggests that young adults work at a start-up early in their career. The constant collaboration is unmatched, and you are exposed to the many different aspects of building a company from the ground up. Most start-ups also have a laid back atmosphere, which can help ease the transition from college to the working world.

Though Meghan didn't always know about the benefits of start-ups, she quickly became a fan once she started working for ZinePak. Now just after a couple of years with the start-up, Meghan is the New Business Manager. If the promotion wasn't exhilarating enough, ZinePak was featured on Shark Tank and funded by Lori Greiner and Robert Herjavec in April 2015.

The combination of having a laid-back but results driven culture immediately confirmed that Meghan had made the right choice in leaving her corporate job. Meghan, working at a growing start-up seems like the right career choice for an ambitious, hard-working recent graduate.

If you have read more than a paragraph of this book, then you know that there are a plethora of career options out there. The idea of individuals having limitless options for their career path is a new concept. This is disrupting the conventional methods and messages around career development. While some institutions are adapting and providing a well-rounded program that highlights the many alternative career paths noted in this chapter, many universities are stuck in the past. It puts a lot more responsibility on you to explore your options.

This chapter included stories of solopreneurs, wellness coaches and even individuals in more traditional careers like education that have found happiness by following their passion for running. If you take anything away from this chapter, I hope you have learned that there is no "one right" way to find your niche. Looking outward is not easy. It is much easier to follow the pack and go through the motions like everyone else. However, like most things in life, those that are willing to put in the effort and think for themselves are also the ones that reap the rewards.

Chapter 5
Digital Tools that Have Changed the Game

Social media is a game changer for job seekers. We spend a lot of time talking about what not to post on social media, but this chapter is more about how you can leverage these tools to change your life and find your niche. The truth is that 68 percent (that is more than two thirds!) of hiring managers are hiring someone because of something they saw on social media.[xxii] This is incredible news! Social media tools are free, and if you can use them correctly, you can bypass gatekeepers, land your dream job and connect with influencers in your industry. The following stories will share the stories behind the statistics, and inspire new ways of thinking about using digital tools to find your niche.

I remember Wednesday, March 27, 2013 vividly. I was sitting in my office at Rutgers when my phone rang. Even though it was a non-Rutgers number that I didn't recognize, my gut told me to answer it.

The young man on the other end introduced himself, saying he was given my name by a former FDU friend of mine, Joe Paris, who now works in the admissions office at Temple University. While visiting Temple in search of the perfect graduate program, he told Joe that he was unsure if this was the right program for him, and what's more, he was still unsure of his career path. That's when Joe pointed him in the direction of The Niche Movement.

This gentleman's name is Shyam Bhoraniya.

When Shyam explained his story to me on the phone, I was immediately impressed by his ambition. Not only did he take the initiative to look up who I was, but he found my number, and called me. Most importantly, though, he didn't wait to take action.

When we talked face-to-face, I could see the passion in his eyes — he wanted to make a difference in the world. Shyam shared stories of how he traveled to India to help young children, what he wanted to accomplish in the field of social work, and what he was doing to motivate others. I shared my vision to end employment unhappiness for college students and my work with The Niche Movement. The intent behind our respective visions resonated deeply with each other.

As I drove home that evening from the initial introduction with Shyam, I knew that there was a reason I picked up the phone earlier that day. Meeting Shyam led to a plethora of opportunities for both us and our projects.

A week after our initial meeting, Shyam and I spoke again and I mentioned what I was doing with the 6-week Niche Movement cohort. I explained that last week's focus was on motivation and following your passion. Shyam revealed to me his own passion project, called Motivate My Day, a daily newsletter to inspire others. I invited Shyam to do a guest lecture on motivation, and he blew me away with his advice on how to get through the "gatekeepers."

Gatekeepers, in the world of job hunting or launching your new initiative, are the people or things that control access to something or someone in the process of getting noticed. In Shyam's world, there are no gatekeepers. This is the mentality you need to integrate into your life.

In another example from Shyam's world, in the spring of 2013, I was introduced to WOW Talks, a community of people who are passionate about what they do and are given a platform to share those passions (think TED Talk style, but 10 minutes or less). I bought a ticket to the event and later found out that Shyam was planning to attend as well; he had already introduced himself to the event founder/organizer and was able to assist with the event and build relationships with the speakers. Infused with inspiration from that first event, Shyam networked and planned a WOW Talk event of his own with a focus on Education and Start-Ups where I had the privilege of speaking.

There are very few people I know that are as great at getting through the gatekeepers and connecting with others as Shyam. He sees no boundaries between himself and others, no matter who they are or what their position is. When Shyam was given my name and told about The Niche Movement, he found my number and called me; others in the same position would have simply sent an email that only would have been lost in my inbox. With the resources and availability of digital identities and interests, it's easier than ever to find a way to contact someone, build a rapport and get noticed.

Send a note through LinkedIn, Tweet at someone, find a phone number and give him or her a call. Be persistent and genuine in your contact, and most importantly, don't be afraid of the gatekeepers, because with Shyam's attitude, they no longer exist.

Leveraging digital networking tools to build rapport and your personal brand is part of many success stories in this book. While many educators or parents just assume that every young person is online and a savvy digital native, I know better. I meet many students who have little to no online presence, and even more who have a lot of questions about how to best position themselves online. For instance, when I first met Nikki Uy, she had a brilliant resume, but hadn't established herself online.

On paper, she was an excellent candidate with extracurriculars that included leading a group of student volunteers to teach ESL, being a member of her school's Chapel choir, making the Dean's List and being a part of the peer educator program. Yet, if you searched for her online, your search would come up empty.

Nikki wasn't on Twitter or on LinkedIn, and she had only reactivated her Facebook to join The Niche Movement cohort group. Here was a young woman who had significant accomplishments in the real world, but was virtually un-findable.

This happens to far too many student leaders and even professionals in the job market. You should know that when employers look at your resume and then subsequently search you (on Google, Twitter, Instagram, etc), finding nothing is as bad as coming across all of your not so innocent pictures from your freshman year of college. This is why producing a strong digital identity is a critical component in finding your niche.

The first thing I did was advise Nikki to give Twitter a chance. She created a complete account and we set a goal for her to tweet at least once a day. After identifying hashtags and other users relevant to her work and future, Nikki was able to see returns on the power of digital networking and advantages of putting herself out there.

In 2013, Nikki wrote a follow up post for The Niche Movement blog, where she shared her experiences connecting with other speech therapists and graduate students, and became reassured that there was in fact a high demand of work in her chosen field. Nikki said, "These sort of connections, simply through reading Tweets, have reaffirmed what I want to do with my life." That is how powerful digital tools can be for students when they understand them and learn to best put them into action.

Nikki went on to create an about.me page and start a blog where she documented her life, photojournalist style. Her new passion for photography and documentaries coupled with her experience blogging, led her to her next opportunity. As many students do, she spent one weekend indulging in a Netflix binge. During her marathon, she watched *Shelter Me*, a documentary series that celebrates shelter pets with positive and uplifting stories; this inspired her to reach out to the Shelter Me creators on Twitter. She sent them a direct message (DM) expressing her interest in the project and asking if she could help in any way.

She didn't hear back right away, but that didn't discourage her. Two weeks later, she sent a second DM and soon heard back from the director via email. The documentary was scheduled for a shoot later that week and needed a video production assistant for three days. Nikki jumped at the chance, even though her video experience was limited. She learned how to fill the production assistant role and worked with an incredible crew who had also worked with MTV, The Travel Channel and National Geographic. All of this from one Tweet — how incredible is that?

Though Nikki didn't immediately change her life plans based on this experience, it still left a lasting impression on her. As she says, "I basically found another niche."

While Nikki's story is an incredible one, the outcome is not that unusual for those who utilize digital tools and who are willing to push boundaries. The reason this story may seem unrealistic is because not many students are taught how to use these tools to connect and amplify their message. I encourage you to go out and use your social media accounts to connect with others who believe what you believe.

The following stats provide some context for individuals who are interested in how their online presence impacts their career development and/or job search.

- 93% of recruiters are likely to look at a candidate's social profile.[xxiii]
- 59% of millennials said that an employer's provision of digital technology was important to them when considering a job.[xxiv]
- 29% of job seekers have been contacted through social media by a recruiter at least once.[xxv]
- More recruiters react negatively to profanity (65%) and grammar and punctuation errors (61%) than to references of alcohol use (47%).[xxvi]

These stats paint a picture. We know that almost all recruiters are looking at social profiles, and almost a third of all job seekers are being contacted by recruiters via social networks. Watching your language and being thoughtful about grammar in your posts is a great first step when working to clean up your online presence.

Not everyone, however, is using digital media to land their next job. There is an incredible revolution underway in the current job market. There are more entrepreneurs, freelancers and contractors than ever before. In fact, it is projected that 40% of the workforce will be made up of these types of workers in 2020. This next story is an astonishing example of how one can use digital tools to follow her passion, and make a living doing what you love.

Have you ever met someone who lives her passion? Literally, someone who wakes up everyday and everything she does is aligned with a purpose she cares deeply about?

I've met a lot of people who live and breathe their passion, but one particular person comes to mind. Her name is Amanda Morrison, and she is the founder of #DontSitHome.

Yes, take out your phone and do an Instagram or Twitter search. That's all Amanda.

Amanda must have woken up one day and decided she was sick of seeing people sit home in one of the most culturally rich cities in the world — New York City. She decided she was going to use social media and her passion to show everyone all of the amazing things that happen in life when we make the choice to "not sit home." After that, the beta version of what is now #DontSitHome was born.

Before Amanda had this life-changing revelation, she was an Intellectual Property Coordinator at a prestigious news gathering organization. From the outside looking in, you would see that Amanda was only in the beginning stages of a long and successful career. However, when she moved to Hoboken, NJ, something changed for her.

In her circle of friends, she was always the one coordinating fun outings and sharing the up and coming events happening in the greater NYC area. Everyone around her would ask, "How did you know about that?" or "Wow, that's awesome! I never would think to do that." Amanda started to think about this feedback and drum up some ideas that matched her adventurous lifestyle and passion for meeting new people. In October 2012, right before Hurricane Sandy, Amanda launched her blog and shared her first post on Don't Sit Home.

Finding deals, events, and the newest hot spots came easy to Amanda. Over the next few months, Don't Sit Home continued to grow quickly. She volunteered for the Hurricane Sandy clean up and utilized her Facebook and Instagram accounts to provide real-time news and updates to her followers, yet another testament to the advantage of social media.

Within a few months, Amanda became known as the Don't Sit Home girl. The amazing thing is that Amanda was building something bigger than herself, all while working full-time. Her evenings and weekends were spent living life and finding the next experience to share with her followers. She may not have realized it at the time, but Amanda was on the verge of disrupting one of America's oldest traditions: old lifestyle and entertainment publications. She reinvented the way young professionals find out about things to do and places to go in NYC and Hoboken.

The biggest news of Amanda's journey so far came in May 2014, when she ripped off the proverbial Band-Aid and quit her prestigious job to launch Don't Sit Home full-time. I know it would be naive of me to assume that every single day is perfect for Amanda, and filled with fun. I know what she is doing requires a lot of hard work, dedication and momentum, but like most experts, Amanda makes it look easy. She is proof that you can love what you do and actually have a blast doing it. And that's what has made the Don't Sit Home campaign so successful: Amanda's genuine passion for opening people's minds to experiencing the world around you.

Everyone says follow your dreams and do what you love; heck, I even say that! But Amanda is doing more than just telling; she's showing us how to make it a reality. Just as Nina Duong showed us to trust our gut and take a leap of faith, Amanda inspires us to do the work we love.

In my line of work, I often meet young people that don't think it's possible to start your own business or follow their passions. Next time you doubt yourself, think of Amanda. If you have an idea that is new and creative, and you are passionate about that idea, then go after it!

Know going into it that you will put in a lot of hours, many of them unpaid with little immediate return, but if you are willing to work hard, then there is no reason you should give up on an idea before it even has the chance to breathe.

These stories are empowering and represent the new economy. Social media has opened doors that never existed before. As you are about to learn, even something as simple as a slice of pizza paired with a passionate go-getter and an Instagram account can spark a movement.

Francisco Balagtas took what he calls the "unconventional 5-year route" through college even though this has become more common and acceptable nowadays. Immediately after graduation, he relocated to the state of Vermont where he followed his passion, not a career move, to work in the snow sports industry. After working for Burton Snowboards managing a retail operation in Vermont, he then decided to move back to the New York City area for a change of pace, but ultimately regained his footing back with Burton managing inventory and logistics distribution within their NYC flagship store.

However, his true love started at a very young age when Francisco realized his love for pizza. So when a close friend challenged him to eat at every dollar pizza location in New York City within two years, Balagtas happily (and hungrily) embarked on a feasting quest. With the need for a systematic way to record his project, Balagtas turned to social media and decided Instagram was the best platform. Dollar Pizza Slice NYC was born in August 2014. What started out as a simple bet later turned into a life project and successful side-hustle for Balagtas, whose challenge has landed him airtime on

Good Morning America, First We Feast and WPIX Channel 11 News, among others.

With more than 5,300 followers on Instagram, his social media strategies have been the leading factors in projecting his story to a global audience. Balagtas studied his target audiences and their social media habits in order to amass followers for Dollar Pizza Slice NYC. In fact, his project's first boost came when Condé Nast's Traveler magazine account featured Dollar Pizza Slice NYC on their "Follow Friday" (#FF) post and called it their new favorite pizza account. Soon, the story was picked up by other media outlets and the followers came right along with it.

Though his success largely came from smart, intentional social media strategies, Balagtas is a big proponent and true believer in the power of word of mouth. In order to break through the noise and separate yourself, you have to actually physically talk about your vision. In fact, Balagtas landed his first interview after chatting about DPSNYC with someone who connected him with First, We Feast. You never know who someone knows or who you are actually talking to. Speaking with people offers a great opportunity to discuss your passion and plug your side hustle in general conversation.

Balagtas encourages proactivity, passion and growth in everything. In his case, it meant hashtagging his brains out in order to get DPSNYC noticed. It even meant purposely taking a detour during a date so he could secretly stop and do a review. Whatever it takes, right?

For others, that means three things:

First, it means accepting that no one cares what you are doing. In these initial stages of a project or goal, it means you're doing things the way you want to do them because you're the one who is interested. However, as your project develops, there is always change and progression that you have to roll with. Nobody ever did it correctly from step one.

This is where growth comes in. You should always be challenged and you should never be content, he suggests. Allow yourself to fail and try to find out what you're good at because along the way, you're going to realize some things you're terrible at and other things that make you feel like a rock star.

Lastly, it boils down to passion. Passion allows you to fail. It allows you to explore. Having passion means you believe in your project because if you don't, no one else will. Passion makes doing the research and separating yourself from competition worthwhile.

While the pressures of finding immediate success as a young professionals can be intimidating, find relief in knowing that a side hustle can act as an outlet where you can make mistakes, explore and gain experiences. It can give provide perspective on just what it's going to take to find your niche.

Here are some tips from Francisco on how to turn something viral:

1. Believe in it - If you don't, nobody else will.
2. Talk about it - Word of mouth
3. Hashtag - create something unique to you but also will get you out into the open

4. Target your audience - when is audience mainly viewing social media, how/when do you capture them
5. Know your copycats- there is always someone out there doing something similar, separate yourself from them

Whether you're just starting out on your own business (or side-hustle) or you are working as part of a team in your job, you deserve to be noticed for your talents and work ethic. First thing is first: Top producers go public with their ideas.

The top producers in your office, industry and/or organization are good at this, and it doesn't even have to be a grand idea. They use this tactic to maintain an exercise regime, get their biggest goals accomplished or even to accomplish personal goals like volunteering for a charity. Below are a few unique ways that you can start using to accomplish all your hopes and dreams.

Give your big idea a digital presence.

You can't just pencil something in on the Internet; everything we put out there is written in digital ink for all to see. Here are five ways you can give your big idea web presence, and be on your way to accomplishing your biggest goals.

• Have an entrepreneurial idea? Create a Kickstarter for it. If people buy into your idea, it forces you to create it. More tips on Kickstarter at the end of this chapter.

- Have a bucket list? Create a blog post for it. Type up your 15 bucket list items for the year (or month) into a blog post and share it with your network. When you do this, it becomes a great conversation piece with your friends because it gives them an insight into your life; now they want to know which ones you finished or which ones they could do with you.

- Have a big hairy ambitious goal for this year? Document your journey of accomplishing it on Instagram or Snapchat. Create a hashtag for your goal and share your journey with friends and family. For instance, if you want to run a half marathon, create a hashtag like #RunKevinRun or #KevinRunsAHalf. Every time you train, you can take pictures, or share an update about how much closer you're getting to your goal. You won't be able to back out of that because everyone will be asking you when it is and which one you're doing!

- Have an event idea? Create a Twitter handle and website for it. With resources like Wix and Squarespace, creating a website should no longer be an excuse or something you are not technically skilled at. Just like Amanda's story, you don't need to know much to do this, you just need a vision, consistency and something interesting and people will follow. Once you sell that first ticket, the rest is history.

- Trying to finish a book or novel you started writing last year? Create a pre-sale page for it on Amazon. If you're unfamiliar with Amazon's self-publishing options, check out CreateSpace and prepare to be amazed.

Picking that public deadline for your pre-sale page will motivate you to finish that darn book.

The truth is…most of us don't get around to accomplishing some of our biggest goals and aspirations. Because we can rationalize it with ourselves, we make up excuses not to do it. Many friends and colleagues have asked me, "How do you have the time to do all the stuff that you do?" Truth be told, it's not even really about having time on my hands, it's because I like to share my ideas aloud and I take that first step.

Top producers don't wait until something is perfect before they share it with the world; instead they share that vision immediately and allow people to join in to help them create it. We get much more done together than we ever will alone. Share your ideas, and accomplish more. Trust me, you'll find the time to make it all happen.

When I present to students on this very topic, I encourage them to get on LinkedIn and Twitter so they can build a network before they need it. I encourage them to use Meetup and Eventbrite to search for events and Meetups going on off campus. Student entrepreneurship is skyrocketing thanks to tools like Indiegogo and Kickstarter.[xxvii]

I met a young individual that has built an entire photography business because he created a YouTube channel where he shared photography tutorials. People loved his tutorials so they hired him to shoot their product videos, events, and teach them photography. There is no excuse anymore for not chasing your big hairy ambitious goals. It's an exciting time to be a young person. Imagine how much you can accomplish in your 20's? It's pretty fantastic.

Another example of building a following while using digital trends is Nicole Booz. At the time she started GenTwenty, her Tumblr account had over 1,000 views per day. Some of the initial contributors to GenTwenty even began as Tumblr followers. Within less than a year of launching the blog, Nicole and her team had over 100,000 viewers reading the site's content. Having built a following on two different platforms, Nicole offered some words of advice about how to create your own platform and community.

The first step, of course, is getting started. "Nobody starts with a really nice looking website," she says. "It's pretty basic because nobody knows what they're doing. So you can't go into it with the expectation that it's going to be a giant, beautiful thing where hundreds of people are going to come and leave comments every day."

While getting started is possibly one of the hardest things to do, it's also important to be consistent, as your audience and viewers are depending upon your content. Authenticity is also vital to the success of any platform. Though it's hard to connect with people online, your personality and idiosyncrasies should shine in your content, whether that involves pictures, blog posts or videos. Don't do or write something simply because you think it will build up your readership. Do it because you believe in it!

A third tip Nicole suggests is connecting with other bloggers, videographers and industry leaders in your field. Consider it virtual networking! These people will support your platform and vision, as strongly you believe in theirs. Participate in the conversation, and learn about those who are interested in the same things you are. Bonus tip, don't forget to find out how you can help those that help you and return the favor.

Being a college student in the 21st century has both drawbacks and major benefits. College is a place where students learn who they are, and much of that learning can come from the mistakes we make as well that experiences we have. Unlike the experiences of most of us, this generation is living and learning in front of a big online audience. There are some drawbacks; although, I think with the proper education around digital reputation, these issues can often be avoided. The exciting part about being a college student today is that digital tools level the playing field a tremendous amount. With social media, anyone with an idea and a social media account can start a movement if they are willing to put the time and energy into it.

Entrepreneur, thought-leader, and author of Four Hour Work Week, Tim Ferris published an article after interviewing a handful of successful Kickstarter campaigns in early 2012. What he found is that preparation is key, just like a chef who spends more time preparing his menu, kitchen and ingredients than he does actually cooking. Below you will find tips from Nathan Resnick, a 21-year-old college student from University of San Diego who has already run three successful

Kickstarters.

1. Prepare
   a. Know Your Goals
      i.   What do you want to accomplish with your campaign?
      ii. Will this be a one-time project or are you trying to utilize your crowdfunding campaign to launch a company?
   b. Have a Clear Message
      i.   What should people know about your project?
   c. Organize Your Launch
      i.   Who is going to handle what?
      ii. Includes: PR, customer care, updates, and more.
   d. Production
      i.   How are you going to actually fulfill your project?
      ii. If you are producing products, know how you are going to do this before you launch.
2. Launch
   a. Spread the word—inform everyone you know that you have launched.
   b. Follow up with media outlets—contacting them once is never enough.
   c. Keep everyone updated—let people know how your campaign is doing.
   d. Ask people to help you spread the word—forwarding your email or sharing your project on Facebook can really go a long way.
3. After Launch

a. Congrats—thank everyone for their support; crowdfunding is about the crowd not just you.
b. Keep people informed—every two or three weeks, send an update to your backers, even if you aren't sharing good news.
c. Late fulfillment—this is all right - just be transparent with your backers. The key to crowdfunding is being levelheaded with your supporters.
d. Fulfillment—let everyone know that their rewards are on their way. Get them excited and have them share this information.

Chapter 6

It's Not All About The Job

"Treat your career like a bad boyfriend."[xxviii] Amy Poehler gives this advice in her book, *Yes Please*, and while it may seem weird to include this in a book about finding a career you love, she might be on to something here. Poehler is a big believer in many of the same tenants we write about in this book, as she has reinforced these ideas in many interviews and throughout her book. So why would she tell us to treat our career like a bad boyfriend?

The truth is that your career will never love you back. You will feel rewarded by the good work you do or the times you helped your colleagues succeed, but we can't confuse our experiences with our career. There will be times our career won't be fair to us. Even those that love their jobs have experienced an unfair decision by their boss or the misfortune of being passed up for a promotion for a bad reason. Poehler also reminds us that by treating our career like a bad boyfriend, we are more able to leave a job to find a new one. We're not married to our jobs, and situations can always change. Perhaps you are reading this book because you are at a crossroads in your career. If there is anything to learn from the many stories in this book, it's that our "niche" evolves over time and there is always an opportunity to make a change for yourself. You can always break up and fall in love with a new job.

In that same vein, we must remember that finding our niche is not all about the job we do. Many of the people featured in this book have found their niche in a career, and as a result, they are thriving in many other aspects of their life. There will always be work to do. There is a fine line between passion and obsession, and it's important to reflect on our actions. The truth is, if we let our to-do list rule our life, it will catch up with us eventually. It will have an effect on our health, other relationships and our overall well-being. In this chapter, you'll get to know some great people that model this more holistic approach to finding their niche.

My grandparents, Joan and Ernie DeGraw, taught me some of life's most important lessons. I have fond memories of spending Wednesday afternoons with my grandmother at the park, and Saturdays at the hardware store with my grandfather. While I was growing up, neither of my grandparents had retired yet, so they both still worked very hard into their late sixties. Today, leading a busy life means balancing multiple priorities — my grandparents were able to do just that and still spend time with our family and me. But they've taught me much more than that.

My grandfather had an opportunity in his early twenties to open an auto mechanic garage with his cousin. At the time, my grandparents already had one child and another on the way, so my grandfather wasn't able to take the entrepreneurial leap. He needed the job security his current job offered, and frankly, not many people were open to the risk associated with going out on your own 50-60 years ago. My grandfather made sacrifices in other ways. Throughout the end of his career he spent weekdays in Maryland working for his company, only coming home to New Jersey on the weekends. He did this so that he could still provide for his family and reach retirement — a true commitment to both his job and family.

When I went to college, my grandparents were some of my biggest supporters. I was only the second person in our immediate family to attend a four-year school and they dedicated themselves to doing whatever it took for me to succeed. Some of my greatest memories from my college years are the times my grandparents came to visit. They would come down with all the essentials for me and my roommates and take me out to dinner to catch up. As any college student knows, time with family is not only a welcome reprieve, but a valuable asset in making memories with them during the time you spend away from home.

My grandparents are two of the most selfless people I know and have generously helped me get to where I am today. Unfortunately, my grandfather passed away during my last semester of college. This was a hard time for me, but ultimately fueled me to leave a greater legacy at FDU. He is always in the back of my mind when it comes time to make sacrifices, especially during long days. I always come back to his work ethic, selflessness and jovial personality to push me through tough times.

Even today, my grandmother, being the strong woman she is, continues to be there for me. At 78 years old, she still works a few days a week, mows her own grass and continues to visit my cousin Leah, who is now in college, and taking her to lunch a few times a year.

The visits from my grandparents instilled in me the value of making time for the important people around you, especially when it comes to face-to-face visits. As we get older, our lives move faster and faster, and with growing technology, we tend to hide behind our devices. As I carve out my niche, it is a priority of mine to spend time with the people who matter most to me. Dedicate time, whether it's once a day, week or month, to spend time with the people who mean the most to you.

The life of a working mom amazes me. Watching my cousin balance her hectic schedule is incredible. My cousin Jennifer O'Connell Caputo has always been someone I've looked up to and admired — and I'm not just saying that because we're related. Jen has always been an active person, playing field hockey in high school and then in college, with an intense focus on her studies and career goals. Needless to say, she always stands out at whatever she does.

After earning her degree in psychology, she landed a great job with Matlen Silver as an HR recruiter. Her work ethic, personality and talent started to pay off quickly and she was promoted several times early on in her career. Today, Jen has a family with 7-year old twins, wakes up at 5:30 every morning to go to CrossFit and works full-time while making a name for herself at the top of her field. She leads a hectic life, but never fails to make time for family, friends and herself. Jen is giving Sheryl Sandberg a run for her money, trust me.

As I became more involved in college and began to build my resume to prepare myself for the real world, I was always able to turn to Jen for help. She truly was the big sister I never had. I went to her throughout my early twenties for advice on jobs, interviewing, relationships and family. In addition to her caring personality, one of her strengths is her ability to connect with everyone around her and carry on a conversation.

To further illustrate how admirable Jen is, she organized a Hurricane Sandy Relief fund that raised thousands of dollars and collected over 10,000 toys. She did all of this in a matter of four weeks to donate to the community of Seaside Heights and the surrounding districts in New Jersey. She did it all while taking care of her day-to-day responsibilities mentioned above. More than 2 years later, Jen looks back on this time as being one of the busiest months of her life as well as a time when she felt alive and thriving. Her entire life became amplified and whether it was time at work, managing the toy drive or with her family, she felt alive.

As we age, the time we spend with family and friends become more valuable, and there never seems to be enough of it. Just like you, I am trying to live my life to the fullest while defining my own success, making time for my wife, my friends and my family.

When you're trying to find your niche, you may a feel like it's a game of tug-of-war between your personal life and your passion. Take a page from Jen's book and remember that it's okay to be busy, but when you're with your friends and family (especially your parents) you need to shut off everything else and be completely in the moment with them. Practice being present, stop thinking about everything else you have going on for just a second and focus on the person or task in front of you.

Volunteering has several benefits, including a proven positive impact on your emotional and physical health. In addition, it will connect you to more people, and has the ability to improve your level of happiness.[xxix] My cousin Jennifer experienced these benefits and more in her work with the toy drive. In this next story, you'll hear about someone whose volunteering not only positively impacted him and those he helped, but also it had a ripple effect that went on to impact hundreds of lives.

Another long-time friend of mine from high school, Russ Bloodgood, has inspired and influenced me more than anyone knows (including himself). I look up to Russ like a brother and we share many of the same interests and tastes. We also both love golf and have very big ambitions for our lives.

During college, Russ and I would visit each other at least once a month and spent the majority of our college breaks together doing this or that. However, during our junior year, Russ said he wouldn't be coming home for spring break. Instead, he pushed himself out of his comfort zone and did something unconventional — he dedicated his spring break to travel to New Mexico to volunteer along with 14 other students as part of Habitat for Humanity.

When Russ returned, I could see he had grown from his volunteer experience, just like I did after my summer as an orientation leader. He told me about the new group of friends he'd made, the big picture perspective he now had on life and the difference he'd been able to make in the community he volunteered in. Because I looked up to him, not only was I hooked on his words, but curious to learn more.

When I returned to school for my final fall semester, I asked around to see if there was a trip like this that existed or if a Habitat for Humanity chapter had been established at my school. At the time, I turned to Sarah Azavedo and Michelle Brisson, FDU's Director and Assistant Director of Student Life respectively. I told them about Russ' trip and asked if we had something similar, because if we didn't, I believed we needed one.

As it turned out, Russ' trip inspired more than just his own soul. He inspired an alternative breaks program at FDU. His experience encouraged me to assist with several other volunteer initiates and contribute what he shared with me to make these programs successful (more on this in a bit).

While working at Rutgers University, I served as Habitat for Humanity's staff advisor for a year and a half, where their chapter went on to raise $100,000 to build a home for a family in Plainfield, NJ. Had Russ not gone on that trip junior year, none of these things would have happened.

When you're in college, the learning and experiencing you do outside of the classroom is just as important as the learning you do in it. You will never regret lending a helping hand to those who need it. You never know how far your actions can travel and whom they can influence unless you take that first step. You never know who your ideas will connect with. As you're about to learn, when you connect them with the right person, they can have a substantial impact on you and the world around you.

It's funny how someone can give you an inch and then the two of you can go a mile. That's the story of how my friendship with Michelle Brisson began. Going into my senior year at FDU, I knew I wanted to give back to the community that I had called home for 3 plus years, the one that had given so much to me. Inspired by Russ' alternative break trip to New Mexico, I knew I wanted to start an alternative breaks program for students.

When I took my idea to Michelle she was thrilled with the concept. She matched my enthusiasm and vision for the idea and we immediately jumped into planning. I spent many 8-hour days in her office researching sites, filling out applications, developing guidelines, creating participant applications, designing a marketing plan and building a fundraising strategy.

From our initial meeting, I knew I had at least one person in my corner who wanted to make my idea a reality. Michelle's support was the driving force that made the trip come to life. Even though she couldn't make the trip herself, she found us a chaperone, secured us a spot with Habitat for Humanity, assisted with raising over $7,000 in six weeks to fund the trip and gained the necessary administrative approval to send a group of 15 students to Opelika, Alabama for spring break. Her role was not only a supportive one, but a critical one. Without her initiative, the program never would have made it off the ground.

When it was all said and done, just like my friend Russ, Michelle impacted and changed the lives of 15 college students. Because of Michelle's commitment, our group ultimately helped us put the finishing touches on a Habitat for Humanity house in Alabama right outside Auburn University's campus for a woman named Ms. Penny. Michelle continued to run and support the program until she left her position at FDU. Together, we were able to run a second trip the following year with a whole new group that went to Grand Rapids, Michigan.

Michelle taught me the beauty of asking for help. Finding your niche and chasing your dreams will often present you with a heavy workload. Chances are there is someone out there that is not only willing to help you, but who is thrilled to do so.

On the flip side, keep this lesson in mind when someone asks you for help. When someone comes to you, it is your chance to make a difference and to be a ripple effect of positive change in the world. In return, you may just find an incredible mentor and friend.

There are several ways to make the most out of our careers and these stories illustrate the good we can experience when someone takes time to help us or when we volunteer. It's important to also remember the need for balance in our lives. One in six individuals report suffering negative consequences for having a inflexible schedule in their place of work. Furthermore, the millennial generation cites "lack of flexibility" among the top reasons they quit their jobs.[xxx] Balance and flexibility have become some of the biggest issues facing the American workplace in the new millennium. Businesses will have to make changes or they will lose talented people. [xxxi]

According to a recent study done by the American Association of Executive Search Consultants, 85% of recruiters reported job seekers turning down job offers because it wouldn't include enough work-life balance for them. In addition, the study showed that 90% of recruiters are saying this consideration for balance has grown importance among job seekers, and is more important now than it was five years ago.[xxxii]

If you value work-life balance, know that you are not alone. Even though it may feel that way sometimes, many professionals are seeking balance. Finding your niche means finding an organization or a career path that aligns with your values. As Nancy Lyons said in the foreword of this book, values can't just be something we post on a website. Values are living breathing things that an organization will show you in the habits and experiences of the individuals working there. Look for those cues and consider the alignment when searching or reflecting on your current position.

Chapter 7

Surround Yourself With Success

You are a reflection of the people around you. This is just as true for a Fortune 500 CEO as it is for a 7-year-old girl on the playground. The more you surround yourself with motivated people with values, the more you will be motivated and more purpose driven in your work. Surrounding yourself with negativity will have the same effect, and will in turn bring you down. Finding employment happiness often is connected to the colleagues and supervisors you have around you. Sometimes you'll be in a great job, but surrounded by negativity and gossip. Take an inventory of the people around you, and reflect on which individuals might be bringing you down. Find people that will contribute positively to your life. In this chapter, you'll hear about a few people that have impacted my life and others that have benefited from being surrounded by success.

I am a big believer in exposing college students to real-world experiences. Throughout my college career, not only did I have great mentors like Michelle Brisson, but I was lucky enough to have two amazing professors that followed the same empowering belief: Ann Huser and Hart Singh.

Ann Huser and I met during the fall semester of my sophomore year when I was enrolled in her "Principles of Marketing" class. The course opened my eyes to the power of marketing and helped me declare my major. During every class, Professor Huser would explain how the material we were learning related to real-world experience. She gave us examples and taught us how to apply the principles we were taught. Later, I took a senior seminar with her where we worked with Ciao Bella Gelato Company to create a retail brand extension campaign. The best part about this project was its hand-on nature that provided us with real-world experience in marketing that many students miss out on.

Professor Huser became the advisor to the Marketing Mix, FDU's marketing club that I participated in founding. When our club was only a year old, several of the e-board members decided that it was too soon for a leadership change and that our President should remain the same for the following year. As an e-board member with a whole new outlook on how to improve the club, I disagreed with that.

Instead of sending off a frustrated email at 12 a.m. one night, I slept on it. I emailed Professor Huser the next morning and simply asked her to call me. That decision alone strongly impacted the next six months of my life. When she got back to me, we discussed the ideas I had for the club and why more people (including myself) deserved a chance to run for president. To this day, I know that if I had contacted her with a long, drawn out email filled with late night emotions, the situation wouldn't have had the same outcome. Ultimately, she agreed with me and organized a proper election. I gave one of the best speeches of my life and became the first officially elected president of the Marketing Mix.

My second professor, Hart Singh, taught the Entrepreneurship program. A successful entrepreneur himself, having created innovative software solutions for Intuit, QuickBooks and municipal governments. Every class Professor Singh taught felt like a start-up. The first day of class, the 20 students enrolled dropped by a handful after one glance at the rigorous syllabus. He had high expectations of his students, which included creating a business model and writing and presenting our own business plan, as well as keeping up with weekly reading and writing assignments. As more weeks went by, the number of students dwindled, but I am forever grateful that I decided to stay.

Given the new leadership skills I was learning and the positions I held, Professor Singh's lessons resonated with me on a deeper level, in tune with my new outlook on life. I was a student leader and began to envision myself as an entrepreneur one day. If it wasn't for Professor Huser and Professor Singh, I would never have grown to love marketing and entrepreneurship like I do today. Even though I didn't follow the traditional marketing route, the skills and concepts I learned in their courses have been utilized every single day of my journey.

These two professors taught me to challenge the expectations that people set for me, and always try to push beyond them. They taught me how to set ambitious expectations for myself and gave me the tools to reach them. With a bit of ambition and the skill set, you can accomplish anything as long as you are willing to put in the work. When the bar is set high, hustle to surpass it, and work even harder to set the bar higher for the next person in line.

If you're a passionate person, there will certainly be days where you want to fire off that email out of frustration. That's okay! But if you have something meaningful and constructive to say, hold off. Pick up the phone, or better yet, meet with the person face-to-face. You'll be surprised at how positive the outcome can be with a levelheaded dialogue.

In her book *Is Everyone Hanging Out Without Me,* Mindy Kaling describes her college experience with the following sentiment, "I was freakin' Jaws in a community swimming pool."[xxxiii] I wouldn't necessarily go as far to say that I was "Jaws," but by the end of my senior year, I definitely was feeling like a big fish in a small pond. I went to a small private school, and as you can tell from the many stories in this book, I gradually became very involved on campus. By the end of my senior year, I started a Habitat for Humanity program on campus, served as an Orientation Leader, started and went on to lead the Marketing Club, among involvement in many other club and organizations on campus. I was killing it. This elevated popularity and power ruined me. I went on to graduate, and then was left thinking of the good old days on my rotten commute to work a job I hated. Does this sound familiar? Having worked with many college students, I know this story too well.

When I graduated from college in 2006, I had gained unforgettable memories, experiences that prepared me for the real world and a marketing degree. Except, like many others, my first job out of college was nothing like I had pictured. My new "office" looked nothing like Michelle's office that I worked out of at FDU. There were no bulletin boards filled with fliers about upcoming concerts and festivals on campus. My office was more like the solitary confinement unit in a jail. There were no windows, just florescent lights. I couldn't walk to my office like I did in college. Even worse, I wasn't walking distance to all my closest friends living in a beautiful on campus apartment (one that would have cost thousands a month in New Jersey). After college, I moved home with my parents, and had a 90-minute commute in one of the most heavily commuted areas in the United States. All of this misery to make "intern" money with the lack luster promise of a potential full-time job. It was definitely not the post-graduation "real world" I had dreamed of, nor was it as exciting or motivating as the passionate work I had done on campus.

As May turned into June and June turned into July, I realized life was slipping by me at 23 years old. I tried to look at the positives, like being accepted into a masters program at FDU, but my company offered no opportunities for financial assistance and no pay increase.

One day in July, I decided to call out sick from work and Courtney and I hopped in her car and drove to New York City. We went straight to Central Park and spent the afternoon discussing and reflecting on my situation. At that point, I realized I needed to leave my current job and decline the offer for the master's program. As great as these opportunities were, I had this gut feeling that they weren't the right paths for me. Instead, I decided to apply to work in any Student Affairs job at any school that I could.

I quickly moved all my co-curricular activities to the top of my resume, as if they were more relevant than my internships – advice I would share to anyone in college. I included my work experience below and started to apply for entry-level jobs at universities from Boston to North Carolina. After weeks of frustration and coming up empty, I found a position as the Coordinator of Recreation and Special Events at Centenary College in Hackettstown, NJ. I applied, interviewed twice and miraculously landed the job with the experience I gained in my undergraduate journey. I felt inspired again and finally saw all the hard work and long hours starting to pay off.

The is where I met one of the top three supervisors I've ever worked for — Kristen McKitish, Centenary's former Director of Student Activities. One of the best things she did was to simply build rapport from the beginning and then continued to trust me. During my first week, she asked me to stay late for one of her evening events. Being new and eager, I jumped right in and was able to connect with students. Kristen gave me a sense of responsibility right out of the gate, which was a crucial component to growing my confidence in the position.

She helped me meet the right people on campus, navigate my way through the politics and red tape and offered her help only when I needed it. She would always say, "You good, Kev-O? If you need my help, just let me know." There were certainly times when I needed her help or assistance, but for the most part, the show was all mine.

When I look back on that job, the environment Kristin created was all about autonomy and not taking things to seriously. Yes, I was hired to run and grow Centenary's recreation department. However, I also volunteered with the Hurricane Disaster Relief trip, helped bring the first ever Student Leadership Retreat to campus and created marketing strategies for the entire Student Life office. Between the experience and right timing, I was encouraged to go back to school for my master's degree in leadership, and to do it while I was working full time at Centenary College.

Kristen was able to strike the balance between knowing how to work with everyone, being a leader and still keeping her head down while helping those around her. She taught me how to supervise students and build a respectful rapport with them, even though I was only a few years older than most of them. She showed me the importance of creating an environment where your people can thrive. She taught me how to trust in others and where the sweet spot is between micro-managers and the missing-in-action managers.

If someone gives you the opportunity to build something from the ground up, take full advantage of it. Use it as a chance to figure out your niche and build upon that experience. I have seen too many people start a job in an autonomous work environment and run away because they are afraid to mess it up. Believe in yourself and make the most of these opportunities.

If I have learned one thing from being Founder of The Niche Movement, it's that whether you like it or not, you'll need to be comfortable and good at speaking and writing to be successful. If you care about something and your job is to get other people to care about that issue, you will need to write about it and speak about it. While I hated how writing intensive my graduate program was at the time, I am thankful for the opportunity to finesse these skills. I was lucky to have a faculty member in that program that could really help me articulate my values both written and through presentations.

My master's program was a rigorous one and Advanced Written Communication eventually became a program requirement, and for good reason. The program was so intense that after I competed my degree, my portfolio of the papers I had written during that time filled a four-inch binder. When I began earning my master's degree in Leadership, the first class I enrolled in was Advanced Written Communication. A man named Jeff Carter, a retired police captain who was working towards his doctorate and doing his dissertation on Toxic Leadership, taught this course.

Jeff Carter was by far one of the best professors in the entire program. He was down to Earth, treated us like real adults and was one of the most efficient and well-prepared professors I've ever had. On the first day of class, he told us we would be writing a 20-30 page paper that semester, but instead of leaving it up to us, he taught us how to research, write in APA style and how to effectively manage our time with our writing so we wouldn't find ourselves waiting until the last minute.

In addition to his effective teaching skills, he never failed to capture my attention during every session of each of the three courses I took with him. He matched the style of Ann Huser and Hart Singh, two of my favorite FDU professors, because he brought real-world examples to every class.

Much of what Jeff Carter taught me has become the framework for my personal leadership style: Relational

Leadership. Jeff brought his whole self to every class. He engaged with his students and relayed his passions about leadership to us while creating an environment where we could thrive.

When you are in a position of leadership, don't stand on a pedestal. True leadership is not about giving direction but about leading by example. People want to connect and relate with you, so give them stories and the chance to do so. Open yourself up to critique and criticism, just like your students and listeners are doing.

Learning how to write and present is extremely important to those who are carving out their niche. My advice to you is to seek out opportunities to fine-tune those skills. Whether it is participating in a TEDx event, sitting on a panel, or presenting at your next meeting, the opportunities are there, just waiting for you to take advantage of them. Remember — building your skills to share your message with the world is just as important as figuring out what that message is.

If you sat through any career development workshop, you have heard about the importance of building your network. It's true a network is necessary. Turns out that 80 percent of all jobs are not even advertised![xxxiv] If you are sitting on your couch perusing the Internet for jobs, you are missing out on 80 percent of the opportunities out there. This is why a network is a critical component of any career development strategy. The one thing we are not telling young people in these networking workshops is that you can't wait until the job search to build that network. A good rule is to build your network before you need it.

During my two years at Centenary College, my goal was to build a foundation for the recreation department rather than simply create one facet of the program. When researching ways to make this happen, I came across the National

Intramural Recreation Sports Association (NIRSA). I discovered that Rutgers University was hosting a workshop and registered five student employees and myself to attend the event.

Less than a year later, I attended a second event in Ithaca, NY where I brought along four student leaders who had a career passion for campus recreation and fitness. We joined the conference early for the Student Lead-On portion and I registered all of us for the mentor-mentee program. Even though I was attending the conference as professional staff, I still knew I had a lot to learn and could benefit greatly from getting to know more seasoned colleagues in the field. As fate would have it, I was paired with Jess Ward, the Intramural Coordinator at Rutgers University.

Jess' welcoming personality and genuine effort to introduce me to other RU alumni and East Coast-based recreation professionals has been an invaluable stepping-stone to my career and finding my niche. I had the opportunity to work with Jess and other recreation professionals that helped me build my network and gain insight into growing the recreation program at Centenary.

When a position opened up within Rutgers Recreation, Jess helped get my resume to the top of the pile where I was lucky enough to interview for the position. A few weeks later, I found out I unfortunately hadn't gotten the job, but it was okay — I had more experience interviewing at a larger institution under my belt and was able to get my foot in the door.

I sent thank you notes to everyone I met during that process and a few months later heard about another position as Intramural Programming Coordinator. As it turns out, this was Jess' position that was coming vacant as she was leaving for a position at Princeton University. The saying "everything happens for a reason" may be cliché, but I ended being selected for an interview for the new job and landing it after the second interview with Rutgers. I owe a sincere thanks to Jess Ward for always helping me out. My new boss at the time, Paul Fischbach, called to welcome me aboard the day I accepted — a sincere gesture I still think about today.

Paul has been an influential role in helping me find my niche, as we share the same values in student development. In my new role, I was able to combine my passions of programming and development with my knowledge of leadership to facilitate a community where college students could learn real-world skills. Paul always said that we helped bring students together and that recreation just got in the way – something I believe to this day.

Both Jess and Paul taught me that value of having a caring and genuine personality. Networking is a two-fold process — it's not just about who you know but about how you treat that relationship. If you don't know someone, in many cases, it can be very difficult to even get your foot in the door. But with that being said, don't network just to network; being authentic and having integrity when connecting with others is a critical component to building your network.

My relationship with Jess didn't start when I applied to Rutgers and it was never about getting some job. Our relationship started years before a position even opened up and was built on a shared passion of recreation and creating opportunities for students. Take advantage of mentor-mentee programs when you have the chance and professional development opportunities — they are a key component in helping you find your purpose and get to the next step.

When I started at Rutgers, I was nervous about the intimidating nature of starting out in an entry-level position at one of the largest schools in the country. However, my boss,

Paul, did a fantastic job of encouraging me to network outside of our department. I took every opportunity I had to grow my network and enhance my professional development by attending workshops and events to meet other student affairs colleagues.

A few months into it, I met Avani Rana, who was in charge of student leading for Student Life. I shared my leadership background and the initiatives I helped create at Centenary College, which led us to collaborate on projects representing our department. The following spring, Avani invited me to sit on the Rising Leaders committee and lead a module on communication.

I continued to stay involved in Rising Leaders and ran workshops and retreats for students. At the same time, I also became the State Director of the National Intramural Recreation Sports Association (NIRSA) where I sat on various committees and assisted with events. This was me "paying it forward" and truly helping students connect with the right professionals — just like Jess Ward did for me. Professional development is a cyclic dynamic: you start as a new professional, begin to carve out your personal niche, and then help others make the connections they need to find their own niche.

Every year I worked at Rutgers, I had the pleasure of working with great students that were thriving in their roles with recreation, student leadership and NIRSA. But I started to observe something. I noticed that these great students were thriving in college and then after graduation, many of them struggled with fulfillment and finding happiness in their new post-graduation lives.

The conversations of "I think I chose the wrong major" and "I shouldn't have decided to enroll in this master's program" or "I'm bored with my job" were uttered far too often. I would then put my counselor hat back on and try to point them in the right direction.

Ultimately, it was during these 3-4 years that my calling to help students stand out and foster their "real-world" skills to succeed after graduation revealed itself. This became my "why" — the reason I get up every morning and help point students and new grads in the direction of a more fulfilled life.

When I started at Rutgers, I was nervous to be thrown into such a large environment, but it soon became apparent that this is where I need be. I learned how important outreach and exposure are when you are trying to find your niche. Between Paul and Avani's efforts and guidance, I was soon able to make a name for myself based on my talents and skills. The moments I was able to run workshops, facilitate team building during retreats, and present to large groups has been invaluable to my work with The Niche Movement.

Early on in your career, take advantage of the committees or groups available for you to participate in, especially if you are passionate about your job. At times, it may feel like extra work, but in the long run, it just may bring you closer to finding your niche.

In 2010, about a year and a half into my job at Rutgers Recreation, I had already learned how to update our website on the backend, use iMovie to make promotional videos and found new ways to reach our students through social media. In late 2009, Facebook had just turned 5 and new Facebook Pages began to pop up everywhere. Based on my previous knowledge and ambition, I asked to lead a committee to build out a social media presence for our department. After exploring trends, best practices and seeing what else was out there, we launched our Facebook Page for Rutgers Recreation in the spring of 2010.

Mind you, at the time, this was still considered "other duties" and not a core part of my job description. I say this because I want you to realize that these "other duties," that are sometime monotonous and tedious, are not always a bad thing. In fact, it was these "other duties as assigned" that helped shape my own career path.

As I led our social strategy, our director allowed me to recruit four students to join the team. At the time, I had a small outreach plan and not a lot of demand, but one project led to another, and the need for video and photos soon emerged. Over the next two years, this part-time project turned into a department full of social media managers, photographers, videographers and brand ambassadors. This eventually led to the creation of a full-time position to run our marketing and social media. You know that you are carving out a niche when someone creates a position for you.

At the time, this had been one of the biggest accomplishments of my career. It required a lot of hard work, savvy resourcefulness and small wins. Trying to build your niche and make a name for yourself requires long hours, extra effort and the desire to learn new skills.

Don't ever be too good for the "other duties." Be the person that takes those additional tasks and makes them awesome. It's so important to be firm in your vision but flexible in your path and methods. There were times when I would have loved to have more resources than I did, but that wasn't the case, and I couldn't let that stop me. Keep focused on your vision and find a way to make do with the cards you've been dealt.

Even with my can-do attitude, there is no way I could have managed this without the help of three special co-workers: Kristin Pettis, Kate Quinlan and Meredith Stille. Kristen showed me how to be selfless. No matter what she had going on, she always made herself available to help others, and always did so with a smile on her face. Kate taught me tenacity. She is the type of person who gets an idea and does whatever it takes to execute it. Finally, Meredith taught me what it takes to truly be there for someone. When one of our student employees had a family tragedy due to Hurricane Sandy, Meredith stepped in to help with no questions asked.

These three remarkable women taught the value of dedication to your vision; how to utilize your passion to make a difference in the lives of young adults and to never get caught up in the status quo. They each continue find ways to improve their programs and themselves.

In your own life, look for the coworkers that you are drawn to. Their attitudes and work ethic will inspire you to be the best that you can be. Along the way, I have also found that there will be two types of supporters in your life: activators and cheerleaders. Cheerleaders are great because they are the type of people that will give you an epic pep talk right when you need it. They might share your successes with other friends or they'll be the first ones to like your status on social media. Cheerleaders make you feel awesome! Activators are critical to your success. They are the ones that actually do something about supporting you. This next story about an incredible activator.

During the first few months of The Niche Movement's life, I had a growing number of supporters and advocates that initiated some early outreach. One advocate that really stands out and still supports my vision to this day is Katie Bean. Katie is a friend of my wife, Courtney's, and has been ever since they met in graduate school.

Upon earning her master's degree, Katie moved to Washington, DC in 2008 where she worked as the Assistant

Director of Alcohol and Drug Education for three years. Katie is one of those people who has a huge heart and believes 100 percent in what she does. She has a vision where every college student is properly educated and supported to make healthy lifestyle choices thus leading to a healthier and safer campus for everyone.

Katie is someone that doesn't just talk about change, but creates it. Her mantra is "Be the change you wish to see in the world." After telling her about my ideas, it was only a matter of time before I saw something different from many of my other conversations with supporters…I saw her take action.

When I launched The Niche Movement's first online cohort for college students to help them find their niche, Katie Bean was one of the first colleagues to share it with her network. Not only did she promote it, but also she encouraged a few of her peer educators that were juniors and seniors who were looking for some direction upon graduation to apply to this program. I can't thank her enough for her belief in one of my first initiatives. Because of Katie's support, four students she knew were accepted into The Niche Movement's program. One of her students, Nikki Uy, had the incredible story (shared in Chapter 5) of turning a Tweet into an opportunity to work on a Netflix documentary.

You will always have friends along the way that will listen to your ideas and share their support with you. However, activators like Katie are game changers. She took the conversation a step further by sharing it with her students and supporting their involvement in the cohort. That kind of action-oriented support is invaluable. Having Katie as one of the first advocates of The Niche Movement helped me establish a name for my passion project outside of New Jersey.

The most important advice I can give you when it comes to networking is to put as much work (if not more) into maintaining your network as you do to grow it. The most successful people that I follow are incredible at maintaining relationships. Whether it is "posting it forward" through digital media like giving someone a LinkedIn endorsement, or more traditional methods of calling to catch up with someone or having lunch, these are so important. You will quickly become known as the needy friend or colleague if you're only going to your friends and network when you need something. People help the people that help them. Much like I said earlier about building your network before you need it, you want to focus on maintaining and building better relationships before you need them. My in-laws are an excellent example of this.

I have been very blessed with a family of in-laws who have treated me like their own from day one — sports rivalries aside. My wife's family can be summed up in one simple phrase: they each follow the beat of their own drum.

My parents-in-law are now retired, but despite being at the opposite end of the career spectrum, they have still taught me many valuable lessons when it comes to following your passions.

Don and Colleen, now retired in Venice, Florida, are at the opposite end of the career path spectrum, but they have taught Courtney and I many lessons to help us follow our passions. As I reflect on these lessons, it always comes back to Don and Colleen "dreaming big." Over the last 11 years, I have seen them in their professional element where their work comes natural to them.

Colleen, prior to her retiring, was a dedicated guidance counselor loved by her students and fellow educators. I have seen her truly help her students, whether it be assisting the best and brightest get into the Ivy Leagues or help students with tough circumstances get what they needed to attain their high school diploma. Colleen's resume didn't end when she moved to Florida. In 2013, she obtained her real estate license and partnered with a successful realtor, Judy Mazrin, and the two of them are making quite a name for themselves. See, no matter the work she is doing, Colleen has the skill to care about those around her and build long-lasting relationships.

My father-in-law Don, has a remarkable story. He grew up in Pennsylvania during the great depression where his family came from very little. He worked very hard to attend and graduate from Temple University, where he earned an accounting degree. Don doesn't mention it often, but he also enlisted in the marines as a way to pay for his education. For a few years, he worked for an employer, but in his early 30s, he took a leap of faith and started his own accounting firm. This firm was started the old fashion way: on a napkin and with a firm handshake with his partner. Don never looked back and grew his firm to be one of the best in the Poconos. Needless to say, Courtney and I turn to him for any finance or business advice, among other things of course.

Many people who follow their passions can get too wrapped up and not find time for friends and family. That is not the case for Don and Colleen. Since retiring to Florida, I'm convinced they are living a busier social life than Courtney and I. Their days are filled with golf, swimming, dinners with friends and visitors from up north (especially, between January – March). Before they retired, they led the same lifestyle and had several pockets of friends and family they would spend time with. At the end of the day, I'm sure moving to Florida may have been tough, but they had big dreams for how they wanted to spend their retirement and so they went for it. Despite this, they still manage to keep in touch with all of their friends and family from up north. Managing these relationships from a distance takes intentionality and effort — two skills that they put into all of their relationships.

My brothers-in-law, Kyle, Brian and Mickey, embody the same quality traits as their parents, and then some. Brian followed in his father's footsteps and went into the accounting business. When I launched The Niche Movement, he helped me register my business and take care of the necessary paperwork to form an LLC. My youngest brother-in-law, Kyle, took his own leap of faith and moved to Australia for work. Moving halfway around the world from everything you've ever known takes courage, a sense of adventure and the ability to roll with the punches.

They all inspire me to dream big and constantly show me the importance of maintaining your relationships regardless of what else is happening in your life. When you're carving out your own niche, you will need to learn to advocate for yourself so that you achieve what you want and what you need. Find the balance between what makes you happy and keeps you on track with following your passions while still keeping up with those who are nearest and dearest to your heart.

When they say the apple doesn't fall far from the tree, it couldn't be more true than it is for my wife. You just read about her family of big dreamers and risk takers, and she has exhibited those traits throughout her career. Courtney got her job working with Erik Qualman, not by looking it up online, but because he Skyped into a leadership class she was teaching. On a whim, she connected with him on Twitter about how her class was reading his book, and he offered to Skype in to talk with the students. When she sent a thank you note, he replied noting he was looking for a "number two" in his company. She loved her job at Rutgers and wasn't even looking to leave. However, her boss told her that if she didn't apply to something like that, then he would. It was too good to pass up. That's the beauty of serendipity. These happy accidents are unplanned but can have a big impact on our life. If you focus on living your life rather than sitting behind a screen planning it out, chances are you will experience more of these serendipitous occasions. This next story truly highlights the influence that serendipitous connections can have on our careers and ultimately, our goals and aspirations.

I met Anne and Mike Howard, of HoneyTrek.com, through a mutual friend, Amanda Morrison, creator of Don't Sit Home and featured in Chapter Five. Though many people find their passion after going through a period of hardship and struggle, some simply decide that the lifestyle they're living is no longer suited for them. That's what happened to Anne Howard. Anne had always wanted to be a writer, noting that she always put "Writer" in the Jobs section of M*A*S*H games she used to play as a child. After starting an internship with InStyle Magazine (packing boxes in a fashion closet), Anne worked her way up through the ranks to become the Executive Editor of various interior design magazines.

After years of hard work and climbing the "corporate ladder," she'd found her niche with design writing. While her position gave her a comfortable corporate life in New York, it also came with it a daily dose of stress and anxiety.

But more on that later.

Anne's husband, Mike Howard, didn't receive his first W2 until he was 35 years old; see he'd never held a conventional job until he was in his mid-thirties, and even then it was only for 12 months total. Mike's entrepreneurial mindset had carried him through the better part of his life by helping him start companies and small businesses. Immediately after college, he and a few university buddies created and sold advertising and tools to magazines, tearing up their $80k offer letters from blue chip companies in the process. He and his friends ran the company, Kiwibox, for 12 years until 2011.

Anne and Mike met in New York City and occasionally took international vacations in and around their work. They both say that the thought of taking a year off of work and traveling the world never crossed their mind during these trips, even though that's how HoneyTrek got started.

Year after year of working, they both succumbed to the "workaholic" lifestyle — working until 2 a.m., chasing promotions and sacrificing their work-life balance in the process.

Anne and Mike's lives changed after Mike took a trip to Oktoberfest for a bachelor party. While in Germany, he met a man who had been traveling the world with his girlfriend for a little more than a year, but only spent about $45 per person per day. Mike's interest piqued because he and Anne had recently been talking about where they were going to go on their honeymoon. Instead of choosing just one destination, why not travel the *entire world* during their trip? Though the idea initially sounded farfetched, they soon realized that there was no better time to complete the journey. Anne and Mike had reached a pivot point — they could either continue making excuses, or start taking steps in the right direction.

After several months of planning, garnering support from their friends and family and transitioning out of their NYC jobs, the pair set off in January 2012, originally planning to only travel for a year or so. Their "honeymoon" wound up lasting 23 months, spanning 6 continents, 23 countries and 203 places!

Mike and Anne currently feel that their "home" is relative, as they don't have a permanent address. At the time of their interview for The Niche Movement, they were living in Mexico housesitting for six weeks!

How could the dynamic duo continue to work after taking an extended vacation from their normal lives? Colleagues asked the same question. Anne and Mike have acknowledged that the job market is not what it once was. People can reinvent themselves at will, learning new skills on the job or leaving the job market altogether and creating their entire career description based on their interests and passions.

The couple's interview touched on many fears that people unhappy with their career situation face. How could the dynamic duo return to their careers after taking an extended vacation from their "normal" lives? Colleagues asked the same question, expressing concern that Anne and Mike would have trouble re-entering the job market after taking a year off, or that they would "miss something" while they were gone. The couple, however, has focused more on what they've gained rather than what they've missed. Mike and Anne feel that they've learned invaluable, marketable skills during their honeymoon, on topics ranging from communication to budgeting to learning how to start your own business. By creating and building the HoneyTrek brand, they've also gained experience in social media and writing.

Networking has also positively influenced their experience, and given them leads to find jobs should they ever want a conventional 9 to 5 again. The couple says that the connections they made while working in New York City introduced them to other connections across the globe.

These friends of friends helped Mike and Anne plan their almost 2-year long honeymoon. Even those contacts that don't produce immediate, career-oriented results can be useful. Mike noted these "invaluable" relationships he's fostered with people that were simply connections of connections provided a helpful shoulder to lean on and words of advice when he needed it.

Meeting new people also forces job seekers to step out of their comfort zone. No matter what, Anne says, don't be shy. A seeker should always go out of their way to introduce themselves to someone they deem interesting, and ask them questions. People love to talk about themselves and their accomplishments. They'll also notice that you've gone out of your way to introduce yourself and talk to them. Greeting someone new at a meet-up or networking event shows that you're bold and willing to put yourself in unknown (and sometimes uncomfortable) situations.

Of course, following your passion comes with challenges. You may not make as much money as you did with a conventional job. That being said, the couple cautions against doing something purely because you'll be making a lot of money. You should do something you love because you love doing it, not because someone tells you that it's lucrative or because you want to reap material benefits. Follow what you love first and the money will follow.

The couple also admit that it can be difficult to get yourself started, take a risk and plunge yourself into the unknown. Anne advises college students and recent grads to "take the leap" and put themselves "into the mix." Putting yourself into a space where value is placed on your interests opens the doors to (sometimes hidden) opportunities. This could mean anything from moving cities, to joining a club or trade association.

A final and important note that they make involves American consumerism. Social media advances this consumerism by instantly "delivering" your desires to your doorstep, in the form of an advertisement on Facebook, or eye-popping photos on Instagram. While it's easy to feel inadequate, Anne and Mike have taken steps to reject these cravings in favor of putting their focus on creating experiences rather than acquiring material possessions. This is just one of the many suggestions they advise for people attempting to follow their dreams or pursue an entrepreneurial goal.

This chapter highlighted many approaches to building and maintaining a strong network. The truth is that relationships get the work done. No one achieved greatness sitting in a room by themselves. Well maybe that recluse author or artist we learned about in high school English class. Aside from the Edgar Allen Poe and Howard Hughes of the world, the rest of us will achieve greatness because we have an incredible network of people that have lifted us up and let us stand on their shoulders.

Hopefully, these stories have destroyed any inkling you had about networking being like speed dating and handing out as many business cards as possible in a one-hour time slot. This is what we call, "spraying and praying," and it is a terrible approach that never works. Instead, we implore you to connect with people that have a purpose or values that align with your own. Build your network well before you need it, and do so in a way that puts more focus on maintaining relationships rather than collecting as many business cards as possible.

Chapter 8

The Ever Evolving Niche

Recent studies have shown that the average person will be making a career change approximately 5-7 times in their working life.[xxxv] It is important to note that this statistic is not referencing job changes, but career changes. The stories throughout this chapter (and many you have already read throughout the book) will give you the personal stories behind this statistic. In chapter one, I mentioned how playing with Legos made me think I wanted to be an architect. When I learned the game of golf I thought I would be a PGA pro. The truth is that our passions and interests often drive our career choices. Just look at Eppa Rixey's story of top-tier management consultant turned craft beer enthusiast and eventually strategic planner for one of the top craft beer companies in the country.

At the age of 26, Eppa Rixey orchestrated a career pivot that drastically changed the course of his life. After graduating from Vanderbilt University with a degree in mechanical engineering, Eppa had his choice of job offers from top-tier management consulting firms throughout the country. He ultimately decided to work for Bain & Company. After a couple of years of working for the company, he was given the opportunity to complete a 6-month externship at the company of his choice. The stipulation was that he continue working for the Bain and Company after the externship was over.

During his first couple of years as a consultant, Eppa spent his nights and weekends immersing himself in the history and chemistry of craft beer. He had a passion outside of his day job that really peaked his interest. So when given the chance to complete a 6-month externship, Eppa began looking for opportunities in the craft beer industry. He was constantly learning about the process of making craft beer and organizing special craft-beer happy hours for his colleagues. He wanted to gain hands on experience in the industry. It took a little bit of curiosity and courage to be able to network outside of his field. However, after contacting a variety of leaders in the craft brew industry, he ultimately wound up connecting with an employee at Lagunitas Brewing in Petaluma, California about the possibility of doing a 6-month externship with them.

At the end of their initial conversation, the employee asked if Eppa would be available for an interview. Eppa being one for not wasting time, fired off his resume immediately, and within a couple of hours had completed his first interview in the same day. He was then referred to the CEO and one of the managers of the finance department. Eppa clicked with both immediately and within a couple of days, he received a phone call.

Lagunitas did not want to hire Eppa for an externship...instead, they offered him a full-time position at the company.

Eppa now had a tough decision to make; should he continue working for Bain & Company, or pursue his newfound love of craft beer. After consulting his girlfriend and colleagues, he decided to move to San Francisco and become Lagunitas' new Strategic Planning Manager. "How could I not take this?" he thought. It was simply too good of an offer to pass up.

Eppa's job offer deviated far off of the 5-year plan he had created for himself after graduation. He originally viewed the 6-month externship as a safety net. He believed that after completing it, he would go back to work at Bain and ultimately get his MBA. Then, after graduate school, he would look into positions in the craft beer industry.

One piece of advice he gives to recent graduates is "don't be too hell-bent on the path." In third grade, he thought he knew what he wanted to do for the rest of his life. He thought the same thing at the end of college. Eppa believes that one of the best parts of having a plan is when it takes an unexpected turn. For some people, once they create a 5 or 10-year plan, they want to continue on that path. Knowing what's coming down the road gives people a sense of security. However, the most intriguing opportunities often come out of the blue.

Making connections with people helps you break into industries with which you may not be completely familiar or have experience. Though Eppa read a lot about craft beer experts, he had no hands-on or formal training in the beverage sector. He began contacting people simply to gain more information about the industry. "Don't go into [relationships] looking for a job," Eppa says. Do it out of "genuine interest" in the field you're pursuing. Eppa tried to understand what it was like to work in craft beer, and wanted to figure out how people got to the positions they held. He wanted to know why they liked their job. Gaining information, instead of asking for a job, helps you build a rapport with the other person and "validate that [the field] is the right choice for you." Hopefully, you'll gain a relationship with the other person. But you should contact people simply asking for information initially.

It also helps to make friends out of your specific field or position. You can learn a lot about yourself, your company and your aspirations by talking to other people with wildly different interests than those that you have. Though these people may not be able to help you find a job at the exact company you want to work at, they may point you in the right direction or offer you another position that will help you gain the experience you need to get to the next level. Talk to as many people as you can and avail yourself to as many opportunities as you can. This will only make you more well-rounded and increase your knowledge about your industry.

Andy Thomas, now CEO of the Craft Beer Alliance, gave Eppa a piece of advice that he never forgot: whatever you Google in your free time, find a way to make money off of it. You'll be taking something you're already interested in and putting the time you spend researching it to good use. Looking at your Google history is a great way to determine what industry you're passionate about. Even things that don't seem like typical jobs can be segued into a profitable career.

Company culture is immensely important to today's generation of employees entering the workforce. Companies in which millennials can thrive and become friends with their coworkers are the ones to draw the most Gen-Y attention. Twenty-somethings want to have a support system and a flexible working environment to match. Both Bain & Company and Lagunitas have a casual, trusting familial company culture. Workers have a support system that helps them along the way. Companies that make merit-based decisions are also attractive for millennials in the workforce. Eppa believes it's extremely important that "you reap dividends for putting in hard work."

When looking for companies with a work environment that "clicks" with your personality, Eppa says, "find a place that feels like home....similarly to if you were looking for a college." Pay attention to stereotypes about certain companies, but be sure to also do your own research, as they may simply be "gross overgeneralizations." Within each stereotype, there is typically a "nugget of truth" that serves as the root of the generalization in the first place.

Navigating the world of job searches and career fairs can be tough, especially if you decide that you want to make an unexpected pivot into a field you don't know much about. Eppa Rixey managed to change his entire career path simply by learning more about the field he was interested in and talking to people that influenced the industry. With the right connections and a strong sense of drive, you can successfully change your current path and begin a career you love!

Sometimes you may have the job you love, but you want to take on more of a leadership role in the company or organization as a young professional. I often advise young professionals to look at their career like it's a pie. Your job is going to take up anywhere from 60 percent to 75 percent of the pie. This leaves anywhere from 25 percent to 40 percent of the pie to play with. How you maximize the rest of that time will define your ability to lead from any position in the organizational chart. For me, it was involvement in regional or state associations as a young professional within my industry.

The more you can leverage that involvement, the more chances you will have to learn and show your leadership potential. In addition, in the 21st century we need to reframe involvement to include online engagement. Whether it's blogging, active participation in LinkedIn groups or adding value to the community of professionals on Twitter, all of these activities will give you additional opportunities to grow your network. I attribute my ability to lead change as a young professional to the time I allocated to these valuable experiences outside of my job. Especially as a young professional, you may find many more opportunities to shine outside of your job than you realize.

I am fascinated with the strategies behind social media, and how brands and people can use it to connect in new and powerful ways. Specifically, I am intrigued by the psychology of how platforms are being used and how millennials are experiencing life in the digital world.

Throughout my 20s, I have spent countless hours finding ways to teach myself technical skills like DSLR photography and videography, Final Cut Pro, Adobe Suite and so on. One of my major role models is Gary Vaynerchuk, author of *Crush It and Thank You Economy*. I did whatever I could to get his attention; our relationship really started when Gary, who has more than a million twitter followers, tweeted me back and invited the digital media team at Rutgers to meet with his agency, VaynerMedia, as part of our training one summer. Eventually, one of our students went on to intern with his company and we attended a second training event, furthering our relationship.

A few weeks into the launch of The Niche Movement, I had the opportunity to interview Gary Vaynerchuk. In addition to Gary's books, he is a tech investor and founder of VaynerMedia and Wine Library. He is an outright hustler and defines what it means to be an entrepreneur in the 21st century.

I only stumbled across Gary a year prior watching one of his keynotes on YouTube. However, after reading all three of his books, watching countless keynotes videos and consuming all his content, he has changed the trajectory of not only my career but also my life.

He is a high profile individual and his time is valuable.

So how did I get 15 minutes of his time to do a podcast interview for my website?

Because communication had been disrupted.

Let me explain. I knew how to break through the noise and get in touch with him for an interview. From finding out who his PR person is on Twitter and emailing her all the way to following up with his assistant (all while emailing Gary as well) at least four times, I was able to secure this interview. Here is a summary what he had to say about the current state of career search, passion and how to be happy.

One of the first things Gary said in our interview was:

> "If a place doesn't make you happy, start looking. You're going to be working more than anything else in their life be happy while you're doing it."

He's right! In fact, the average American is going to work

more than 98,000 hours in your lifetime.

Kevin O'Connell (KO): why do so many people fall into the trap of hating their job or taking the easy way out?

Gary Vaynerchuk (GV): Our society models the go to college, get good grades, get a good job. We don't groom entrepreneurship or support risk taking. Because our parents and family love us, they want us to be safe and take the most attractive or obvious path.

KO: What advice would you would give to anyone who is in college or about to graduate?

GV: Between the age of 16 to 22, take two summers working for the person they most want to be like and   work for free." Reach out to 15-20 people that do what   you want to do at the highest level and say, "I admire what you do and your work. How can I help you?" By doing this, you will standout from your peers and set yourself apart from the pack of applicants, all while building your network and portfolio before you have to search for a full-time job. You don't have to settle, find the right place for you. Whether you create your own niche in your current company, pave a way in your internship or follow your own dreams and ideas, go do it and don't settle.

KO: What advice do you have for those that are applying for jobs?

GV: Do something. Make something. Build something. When you are ready to land an internship or your first full time job, make something tangible that may bring value to that business or person you want to work for. This could be a case study on their customers, assisting bringing in a new client or building an app. You can no longer walk in with just a resume and expect that it's the company's job to pick you. Too many people are sitting and waiting for it to happen. You need to go out and take it. Be proactive.

KO: How do other companies succeed in recruiting and retaining top talent within the millennial age group?

GV: They need to respond to the reality and listen. The reason start-ups are appealing over corporate America is because there is not as much red tape, there is less politics, less tradition; overall, just more Zen."

Gary runs his companies being as transparent as possible and showing effort to all of his employees. He believes this goes a long way. For example, if an employee asks for a meeting at VaynerMedia, it happens immediately. Gary says, "you need to allocate time to everyone in your organization, and if they do decide to leave or find another career path, you should treat them better than if they were staying."

I learned a lot from Gary, and infused many of his lessons in my work at Rutgers. The digital media team at Rutgers managed a handful of social media accounts, but our larger purpose was to serve as the department's voice in a digital space. What I love about social media is that when it is done with intentionality, it can be a powerful and influential connector for your brand.

Much of social media is humanized, from the emotions portrayed to the way we share and interpret information. I realized over several years the importance of continually tweaking your strategy to best connect with your audience. I also realized that social media requires skill that can be taught, especially to 18-22 year old students and young professionals.

If you are lucky, you come across the right person who just "gets it." In 2012, the recreation's media department hit the digital voice jackpot when we hired Rutgers senior Brittney Katz.

In the first decade of my professional career, I have never worked with a student who was as well-rounded as Brittney. She came with the personality, the energy, the work ethic, the brains and the common sense of how to effectively communicate via social media with Rutgers students. Unfortunately, many people who run social media accounts for any business or department think it is as easy as "set it and forget it." This is, however, not the case. It takes creative thought, copywriting skills, design, time and the instinct to know what will resonate with your audience.

Intuitively, Brittney knew this from the beginning. When we launched TweetDeck (a free social media listening tool for Twitter) in the fall of 2012, we encountered hundreds of conversations happening about recreation and Rutgers. Brittney was able to find the best way to reply to these Tweets and jump into conversations every single time so that we could build our audience's relationship with Rutgers Recreation.

When Brittney graduated, she entered into the tumultuous job search of post-grad life. While her first few months were tough, she eventually landed a position with VaynerMedia and had already begun to carve out her niche. Her hard work led to many early promotions, and as this book is being published, Brittney still works for VaynerMedia as their Micro-Content Producer, leading much of the creativity behind the content they create for the Fortune 500 brands that they represent.

Brittney shows us that it is okay to trust college students with responsibility, specifically your brand's social media strategy. This doesn't mean we gave her access to all of our social media accounts in one day; however, with the right training, expectations and feedback, she helped our department break through the static at a large institution.

Many of my colleagues and other business owners are scared at the thought of a college student, let alone an entry-level employee, running their social media and digitally managing their brand. Realize that millennials are immersed in the social media platforms. You will benefit by hiring, training and investing in more Gen Y employees. Conversely, as a student, you will benefit by standing out with a strong, adaptable work ethic and proving that you share and understand the company's goals.

Understanding the environment you thrive in is one step towards finding your niche; understanding why you thrive there is another. Not all the work you do in college or early on in your career may be directly relevant to your niche, but creating a tailored environment for you to succeed, grow and thrive will get you closer to finding it.

When I started at Rutgers, one of my initiatives was to create and expand the community out of the Livingston Recreation Center. Sure, it was easy enough to promote our programs, recruit student employees and lead a handful of staff. The real challenge was to create a volunteer advisory council.

I observed our staff and gradually noted individuals who had the skills and talent I was looking for. I ultimately reached out to Dana Wise, Carlos Correa and Tara Curran because of their love for our recreation center. As the weeks went on, I knew I had made the right decision. They saw my vision, cared about other students and were ready to make a difference.

Dana Wise and I immediately connected when we uncovered that we had both grown up in the same area of New Jersey. Our Tuesday night meetings turned into weekend programs for the Rutgers community. During our most successful event, a 3-on-3-charity basketball tournament, is where I saw Dana truly step up as leader. She was a psychology student and had built an impressive resume by improving her leadership skills and becoming president of our council. She eventually became so involved that she started to second-guess her choice to go in the psychology field. After some long conversations, some tears and some confidence boosting, she ultimately decided to pursue a Graduate Assistantship and attend the NIRSA conference in the spring.

She did everything she was "supposed" to do; she had a strong resume, great GPA, dressed professionally, interviewed well and had a personal touch that made her stand out. Even still, she came home empty handed, with no assistantship and no admittance into a graduate program. A struggle that happens all too often to the best of us.

Dana did do something right, though. Before she boarded the plane to the conference, she struck up a conversation with someone wearing a Cornell sweatshirt. This person was headed to the conference as well and helped put her in touch with a contact at Old Dominion University. While at the conference, she was able to secure an interview for the facilities position.

Even though she came up short, she made a distinct impression. April came and went, and so did May. She graduated thinking the world was about to end because she didn't have a job lined up. After more tears in my office, I encouraged her to keep her head up, keep networking and reassured her that something would come her way.

Sure enough, a week after graduation, she received an email being asked to interview at Old Dominion again for another position. Patience and serendipity matched with her hard work landed Dana a job as the marketing graduate assistant at Old Dominion from the connection she made at the conference. But this didn't end up just being a graduate assistantship. During her time at Old Dominion, she was able to help on an outdoor trip and travel to Peru, she traveled to China as part of a student affairs exchange program, she became best friends with the wife of the university President of Old Dominion and became close with her director, who happened to be NIRSA's next president.

On top of all that, she lived 10 minutes from Virginia Beach while earning a master's degree — not a bad deal if you ask me.

Trust me when I say that all of the hard work and tumultuous emotions that go into finding your niche will pay off. I knew Dana was going to be a great professional regardless of the field she entered into. Now with a master's degree in hand, several major life experiences under her belt and becoming a full-fledged, responsible adult, Dana is the Membership and Marketing Director the YMCA in Wayne Hills, the largest YMCA in the state.

The most important thing to remember from Dana's story (and it very well may be your story someday) is that when an opportunity is put in front you, you must take it, trust it and give it all you have. And when an opportunity isn't there, push your comfort zone, keep moving and work your ass off to find the next door to open.

Some of the most successful people I know, particularly those that have been able to land the jobs we all dream of, are excellent storytellers. Think about it: your job interview is essentially a chance to tell your story. Your resume or LinkedIn profile is telling a story about your career path, talents and skills.

Dawn Fraser is a critically acclaimed storyteller and public speaker. After receiving her Master's in Public Policy from Harvard University, she went on to host and produce Barbershop Stories, a show in which artists from across New York share their own personal tales while getting their hair cut. She's also participated in TED@NYC, writes for the sketch comedy *American Candy* and teaches for The Moth's Community and Engagement Program.

From a young age, Dawn wanted be a professional athlete and win a medal in the Olympics for her exceptional running abilities. Her dreams were shattered when she became injured. Soon after, she began immersing herself in social work and hearing the stories of those in marginalized communities, whether they were people trying to cross the border in Mexico or women behind bars in prison. It was in these situations that she learned about the power of storytelling. Dawn didn't realize *she* was a storyteller until she heard the term coined as an art form while at a conference. As she became increasingly immersed in the scene, she began teaching others how to tell their own stories. She is now an integral part of the storytelling community.

Because of her profession, Dawn has a couple of tips for building and creating your own narrative. Take a look:

- **Explore:** Find out what drives you and what drives other people...you'll learn a lot by going out into the world and talking to people.
- **Tell stories:** The more you talk about a specific event, the more you add details that are interesting and remove parts that you don't need. You find out what people do and don't want to hear about. Try to cater to your audience.
- **Identify critical moments:** What drew you to the profession you're pursuing? Do you remember when you initially considered your line of work? Find the key experiences that influenced you to follow your career path
- **Dig out the narratives:** Look within yourself to find memories that resonate with your current situation.
- **Be vulnerable, but not overly accessible:** Your story should have details, but you don't want to give away too much of yourself during an interview. There's a fine line between sharing and over-sharing. Make sure you're always comfortable with what you're saying. Being vulnerable shows your frustration with a situation, but your ultimate ability to overcome that situation.
- **Focus:** You don't need to tell *every* story that you can remember that led you to your chosen field. Hone in on those that are important.

From her beginnings as an Olympic-bound runner Dawn Fraser's unconventional career path has led her to find her passion and explore her love for storytelling and human rights. She continues to travel the world and teach others how to use their memories to shape their future today.

"Give yourself the permission to explore and the grace to get it wrong." This quote encapsulates Michael DuDell's perspective and advice for millennial college students and recent graduates. He's the bestselling author of *Shark Tank: Jump Start Your Business*, and worked with Seth Godin to start his publishing business. After years of working for various companies including GE, American Express and Kraft, Michael became an entrepreneur and founded Race + Vine, to help companies understand and speak to millennials.

Being the middleman between millennials and large corporations, Michael knows a thing or two about what it takes to get hired. Take a look at some of his tips:

- "Thanks to the Internet, the cost to start something is virtually nothing," Michael says. So right now is the perfect time to draw up a business plan and start hammering out the details of that idea you've always had. However, he acknowledges that some people won't want to immediately jump into a project. "Both [paths] are valid," he maintains. Just know that, while you're young, the risks are low and you have enough time to bounce back from them.
- The college experience is wildly different from what the real world is actually like. And when you're in the university bubble, it's hard to see beyond the tests and papers. Don't be stuck thinking you have to do everything you did in college once you graduate. Marketing majors don't immediately have to get a job in the marketing and communications department of a company. Art majors don't have to go on to become a curator at an art gallery (unless you know you definitely want to!). For example, Michael was a musical theory major while he was at college, a major, he says, "you couldn't trade for a sandwich." Take the skills you've learned in college and apply them to what you want to do at the time. Don't do the thing you've always done just because you've always done it.

- Michael says, "Part of being a young person...is recognizing that we're fluid creatures." Go where your passions are at the time. A lot of people know what they don't want to do but aren't too sure about what they *do* want to do. Understand that your thoughts, dreams and niche will probably ultimately change many times (but more on that later!).
- Resistance and fear set in when people think about questions too broadly. For example, the questions *What do I want to do for the rest of my life? Who do I want to be for the rest of my life* are daunting because you can't predict where life will take you. And declaring a career is "especially scary." It frightens people to commit because they feel like they're committing to forever. Instead, focus on right now. Think: *What do I want to do right now? Who do I want to be right now?*
- "Be aware that the best things in life are never part of the plan." While plans and strategies are important, recognize that when it comes to your career, one thing will lead to the next. One *job* will lead to the next. Trust the process.
- "Everything is about relationships." Networking is key to creating lasting, informative, helpful repertoires with people. Wonderful opportunities come from relationships. Be social.
- Find a way to infuse your resume with your personality. Though Michael personally believes that resumes are "dead" and the solution to the conventional resume will soon enter the job search, try to show the employer who you are as best you can. Be unique. For example, start your resume with a short bio about yourself.
- "Too many people are just nice and pleasant" during their interview. Don't be afraid to keep and use some of your power. When hiring, Michael looks for people who will interview him about his company just as much as he interviews them. Be bold during your

interview, and show the team who you are. Take a look at Contently.com and Fab.com, two companies that may appreciate a bold interview candidate.

- Michael thinks that recent grads entering the job force should be up-to-date on technology, have good communication skills, understand networking, and most importantly HAVE A GREAT ATTITUDE. When hiring, Michael wants to know that the candidate's goals and values line up with his own.
- Never be late! "If you're 5 minutes early, you're late!"

After giving millennials all this advice about how to cultivate their own niche, how does Michael describe his own Niche? "It's always changing," he says. Right now, it involves creating content and helping companies understand millennials. That could change within a year's time, he warns. It seems like we'll have to keep an eye out for Michael's next project!

Michael is an excellent example of the ever-evolving career path that we are talking about in this book. His work is dictated by his passions, and he is able to do that because he has worked hard. He exemplifies the strategies we talked about in previous chapters regarding building and maintaining a strong network, diving into discomfort and leveraging digital tools. While Michael moves from one exciting project to the next, he is focused on long-term goals. Erik Qualman elaborated on this concept in our interview with him.

In his 20s, Erik Qualman considered dropping out of graduate school. As a full-time graduadte student in an unfamiliar region of the country, Qualman felt times were tough. Today, Qualman is in his 40s, and he is a world-renowned author, motivational speaker and thought leader. His expertise lies in digital leadership, trends in emerging technology and digital reputation for brands and individuals.

So what was it that pushed Qualman from potentially dropping out of his MBA program at the McCombs School of Business at the University of Texas to becoming a Forbes Top 50 Digital Influencer? His secret is always considering and keeping long-term goals. When we focus on the short-term game, we are constantly "dancing" and changing direction. It is natural for you to have an idea but that vision is going to quickly change direction. The key is to ask yourself, "is this the direction I see myself going?" Having patience and decreasing your short-term decisions will allow you to stay with your own vision. Not to mention, over the course of time, you have the opportunity to build your network and strengthen relationships with the people you meet along the way. Give them the impression that you are ready to hustle and do the work. At the very least, it's good karma.

Along with focusing on the long-term, Qualman always comes back to how his decisions and actions can potentially benefit others. He says the only thing you can take in life when you're gone is what you've given others. With this mindset, and a little bit of what he calls luck, Qualman channels his team around group success and eliminates the "what's in it for me?" culture. It's not about yourself; it's about surrounding yourself with great people and helping them in turn. Though he admits it can be challenging to scale your work so it's bigger than you — that is, allowing yourself to take a vacation without feeling like the company will crumble — it is important to not become solely dependent.

Everyone needs a circle of trusted friends and colleagues on whom we can rely.

While Qualman's story is one of incredible success, it was no walk in the park. Are you beginning to see a trend here? Becoming an entrepreneur is difficult and requires some serious dedication. He says, instead of following the money, follow the passion. It isn't always easy — but this wasn't made to be easy. As his Michigan State basketball coach Tom Izzo put it, "If it was easy, everyone would be out here doing it." There are talented people everywhere but you have to be willing to make sacrifices and work hard.

According to Erik Qualman, it's important to understand that there is never a definitive, clear sign to follow your dreams. Nowadays, we're never 100 percent sure. But what helps is to ask yourself "what's the worst thing that could happen" and really weigh your options. Realize your strengths, your gifts. Allow yourself some self-exploration to figure out what makes you the happiest and develop a long-term goal that fits that image.

Your career path is going to look more like a jungle gym than a ladder. The ladder of success is an outdated term, because we know that success in today's world often means flexibility in addition to focused long-term goals. Sheryl Sandberg eloquently states in her book *Lean In*, "A long term dream does not have to be realistic or event specific." She goes on to suggest that we all need to have a long-term dream and an 8-month plan.[xxxvi]

This is excellent advice for any one searching for employment happiness. We want to have that dream guiding us. You might even find your dream job description, cut it out and paste it in a journal or post it on a bulletin board. This can be a good reminder of the long-term dream. However, you want to always be reflecting on the 8-month plan. What does success look like for you in 8 months? Are you promoted in 8 months? Are you working for a new company in 8 months? Have you completed an exciting project? These questions will help you come up with your 8-month plan.

Chapter 9:
Concluding Thoughts and Resources

Another example of how social media is making this world a smaller place happened once again in April 2014. After perusing Twitter for businesses and books with a similar mission to the Niche Movement, I stumbled upon Melanie Feldman and Joshua Siva. They are the authors of *BOLD: Get Noticed, Get Hired*. While checking out their Twitter account, I found out they were hosting a workshop at Rutgers University that month. Without hesitation, I reached out and after a few tweets and emails, I was able to meet Melanie at Rutgers (and Josh a few weeks later).

Josh and Melanie are living through many of the same challenges I've outlined in this book, and their frustrations fueled them to create change. They compiled all of their tactics to break through the noise and published a book, all while working part-time. Below you will find a summary of five bold moves they wrote for our readers to help them get noticed during their job search.

1. **Create an "All-Star" LinkedIn profile**

   Many job seekers overlook the power of LinkedIn. If you are serious about landing a job at a great company, you're going to put a ton of work into getting your resume noticed. If you're successful and your resume lands in front of the right person, the first thing they will do is look you up on LinkedIn, so your profile better be first-rate. LinkedIn grades the strength of your profile, so before you start the job search process, be sure that you've reached the All-Star level as a target goal.

2. Use your school's alumni network

HTP! It means *Hail To Pitt* and that is what scored me three interviews after college. I joined my University of Pittsburgh alumni network on LinkedIn, which by the way, allows you to message any person from the group without being connected with that person. I sent each person who worked for a company I was interested in a short message and ended each message with *HTP*. That was all it took to grab their attention. I highly recommend you join your alumni group on LinkedIn. Don't forget to check any internal networks that be set up within your University's websites. This will only expand your potential reach.

3. Tailor your LinkedIn profile and resume to the job you want

The goal here is to ensure that your profile has the content to match the job you want and the terms a recruiter may use when searching for the right candidate to hire. If done correctly, your profile will rank very high in the search results. The simplest way to achieve this is to take a specific job that you want, identify the key words from the job description and integrate them into your LinkedIn Profile and resume. Take a number of the keywords from the job description you're applying for and smoothly embed them into your LinkedIn profile.

4. Get five minutes with someone from the company you want to work for

There are two truths that everyone should be mindful of, especially when searching for a job: flattery works and everyone loves talking about themselves. Don't forget this! So when you've found the company you want to work for, your next goal is to get on the phone with someone from the inside for five minutes. The closer that person is to the internal department you'd be working in, the better, but any inside knowledge is helpful. For the record, this shouldn't be a daunting task.

Draft a short message telling them you are impressed with their background and would love to hear how they got to where they are. Also, ask if they are free for five minutes to jump on a quick call at their convenience. When you get on the phone with them, make sure to actively listen to them, and ask a few questions. I am willing to bet that at the end of the call, they will ask what they can do for you. Voilà, you now have someone from the inside of the company in your corner who can hopefully you get an introduction to the person who can hire you.

5. **Connect with industry influencers and find a way to help them for free**

When focusing on the influential people in your industry, or the industry you're trying to break into, it's remarkably easy to identify what most people are working on. LinkedIn will tell you all that and then some. Justin Mares, author of *Traction Book* is a great example of someone who continuously offers free help and in return cultivates a great connection for the future. After taking a course on Mixergy.com he noticed a lot of opportunity to improve how the company was engaging with their users. Recognizing this as an opportunity to sync up with Andrew Warner, CEO of Mixergy.com, he simply dropped him an email. Free help, and a plan to deliver results: what could be better? Not surprisingly, Andrew gladly connected with Justin on the phone for several calls and eventually reaped the benefits.

Josh and Melanie's book is full of incredible tips and stories just like the ones they wrote about above. I strongly encourage you to read their book as a companion to this one.

Concluding Thoughts

In October 2014, just as The Niche Movement celebrated its two-year anniversary, I listened to my own advice and beliefs that I wrote about in this book and took a leap of faith. I left my job at Rutgers University to launch my company full time. This was a mixture of a calculated risk, courage and trust. I trusted that my work ethic, skills and the network I grew over the last eight years would be enough to make it on my own. As I write the final chapter of this book, I can confidently say that I have found my niche.

Since October, I have built a digital storytelling business under The Niche Movement that works with organizations and individuals that are passionate about what they do, and help them tell their story through photo, video and social media content. In addition to writing and publishing this book, I have delivered workshops and keynotes to a variety of schools and organizations, including Steven's Institute of Technology, University of Illinois - American Disabilities Association and The Jersey Alliance, to name a few. The most gratifying work has been the opportunity to personally help young professionals from all over the United States, and even as far as the University of Calgary and University of Puerto

Rico, find their niche.

Ever since my senior year of college, I knew I wanted to work for myself. Since graduating college, I've been tiptoeing the line of working for others while creating and executing a vision that challenges convention.

While digital storytelling and career coaching may not seem to have too much in common, I found that these two businesses have blended together nicely.

For example, I landed the amazing opportunity to photograph a conference for Venture Well. They are an education tech organization, and I was hired to photograph their conference for disruptors working and learning in higher education. As I photographed this conference over the four days, I met incredible individuals that created co-working spaces on their campuses. In addition, I had the privilege of meeting Barack Obama's former Chief Technology Officer, Aneesh Chopra. It's moments like this that I know all of this will lead to something bigger, and I have learned to have patience and trust the process.

The last six months have been the most rewarding and challenging months I can remember. However, each day has provided a lot of perspective and created a vision for how I can bridge The Niche Movement and my digital storytelling business together. After spending the rest of 2014 interviewing inspirational people for the book, I stumbled upon Nancy Lyons after watching a feature on NBC Nightly News. Through a few tweets and after a connecting over email, I had the chance to interview Nancy. After our conversation she shared substantial excitement and support for this book. She loved the project so much that she agreed to write the foreword for this book without hesitation. Thank you Nancy!

What I have realized is The Niche Movement ultimately is a platform to connect people. Don't Sit Home created by Amanda Morrison and GenTwenty created by Nicole Booz are amazing examples of platforms for passionate communities. I challenge you to find your purpose and create a platform to connect that passion with others. You will be surprised by the doors that will open and the people you will meet. In the end, it will help you get one step closer to finding your niche.

I have three last pieces of advice for you, and they are the following:

1. Take a deep breath and hold on tight

Finding a job you love, or starting your own business, is a long, bumpy and often untraveled path. If you are looking for instant gratification or a quick solution, you are headed down the wrong path. Using the right amount of planning, guts and trust that everything will be okay, you can view this journey as a marathon and not a sprint.

2. Put yourself out there

If you have something you want to share or promote, you have to let people know. Don't forget to have tact and be genuine with a touch of creativity. I have found by just introducing yourself (digitally or in-person) and then leaving with "If I can help, please let me know" or "I admire the work you do, how can I help you?" goes a long way. Remember it may take multiple follow-ups and that is ok. Most of the people interviewed for the book and many of the projects I have worked on came from the simple follow-up, both over the phone and through email.

3. **Care about the people first, work second**

When you're starting out in a new job, career or launching a new business, it is so easy to get wrapped up in administrative tasks, finances, personnel, growth and the like. Genuinely focus on what you love about your job and people will notice.

And remember this:

Do the work.

Ask questions while challenging the status quo.

Add more value than asked of you.

Build Your Network

The 40 plus people listed below are featured in order of how they appear in the book. They are intended for you to connect with or follow should you feel inspired by their story or the work they are doing. If I can facilitate any introduction, please do not hesitate to reach out to me. Be sure to mention the book when you reach out.

Nancy Lyons	http://www.clockwork.net/people/nancy_lyons/
Nicole Piquant	https://www.linkedin.com/in/npiquant
John Giannone	https://www.linkedin.com/pub/john-giannone/a/8a7/a5a
Benee Williams	https://www.linkedin.com/pub/benee-williams/69/260/bba
Amma Marfo	http://ammamarfo.com/
Courtney O'Connell	http://www.courtoconnell.com/
Noah Rosenberg	http://www.noahrosenberg.com/blog/
Nathan Resnick	https://www.linkedin.com/in/nathanresnick
Shaunna Rubin-Murphy	https://www.linkedin.com/in/shaunnarmurphy
Carey Loch	@careyloch
Chloe Alpert	http://www.chloealpert.com/
Chris & Suzanne LoBue	http://clbphoto.com/

Stacy Rinaldi-Campesi	http://slccoaching.net/
Megan Schwab	https://twitter.com/mschwizzle
Nicole Booz	http://gentwenty.com/
Nina Duong	https://twitter.com/sillybanina
Alena Gerst	http://alenagerst.com/
Laura & Joe Jacobs	http://www.sneakerfactoryfp.com/
Laura Zax	https://www.linkedin.com/pub/laura-zax/11/634/863
Kali Hawlk	http://kalihawlk.com/
Meghan St. John	https://www.linkedin.com/in/meghanstjohn
Shyam Bhoraniya	https://www.linkedin.com/in/shyambhoraniya
Nikki Uy	https://twitter.com/makesyousay_uyy
Amanda Morrison	https://instagram.com/dontsithome/
Francisco Balagtas	https://instagram.com/dollarpizzaslicenyc/
Jennifer O'Connell Caputo	https://www.linkedin.com/pub/jennifer-o-connell/0/ba2/984
Russ Bloodgood	https://www.linkedin.com/in/russellbloodgood
Michelle Brisson	https://twitter.com/mlbrisson
Kristen Pettis	https://www.linkedin.com/pub/kristen-pettis/13/129/b54
Kate Quinlan	https://twitter.com/kquin30
Meredith Stille	https://www.linkedin.com/pub/meredith-stille/43/a39/3a4
Katie Bean	https://twitter.com/katiebean2326

Mike & Ann Howard	http://www.honeytrek.com/
Eppa Rixey	https://www.linkedin.com/pub/eppa-rixey/14/359/351
Gary Vaynerchuk	https://twitter.com/garyvee
Brittany Katz	https://twitter.com/IdontgiveaKATZ
Dana Wise	https://www.linkedin.com/pub/dana-wise/85/65/104
Dawn Fraser	http://www.dawnjfraser.com/
Michael DuDell	http://www.michaelparrishdudell.com/
Erik Qualman	http://equalman.com/

Websites

Below are a list of websites, blogs and career resources that I review and share with my network on a daily basis. I highly recommend them. There is no sponsorship attached to this list; therefore, I'm giving an honest recommendation with no strings attached. My goal is that these websites will help in the following ways:

- Help you cut through the noise and get you noticed.
- Provide a platform for you to tell your story or showcase your talents.
- Give you an alternative to the standard job boards and career search methods.

1. GenTwenty.com: A twenty-something's guide to life

2. CareerSushi.com: The Visual Marketplace connects the brightest minds with the most innovative companies.

3. TheMuse.com: Real-time career advice, job board and inside look to the hottest companies hiring.

4. LevoLeague.com: A growing community of professional women seeking advice, inspiration and the tools needed to achieve their career goals.

5. BoldJobBook.com: Authored by Melanie Feldman and Josh Siva — who were both featured in the book — this book will get you noticed and hired — it's filled with tactics that work in today's marketplace.

6. StartUpHire.com: Thousands of startups that are venture-backed, angel backed and bootstrapped all over the world.

7. AngelList.com: Startup hub that is looking for team members and investors — they have the newest jobs that you can get in on the ground floor.

8. BrainGain.com: Helping young professionals find employment and internships with startups in emerging economies and abroad.

9. Idealist.org: The world's best place to find volunteer opportunities, nonprofit jobs, internships and organizations working to change the world.

10. The Niche List: The hunt for the right job requires a lot of time. The Niche List is a weekly-curated list of jobs at companies that twenty-somethings actually want to work for.

Get Involved With The Niche Movement

Become a Contributing Editor:

If you have something to say related to career advice, your life journey or disruptive leadership and unique storytelling, we would love share The Niche Movement with you as a platform to connect with others. Simply email info@thenichemovement.com and introduce yourself and why you would like to write for The Niche Movement.

Work With Us:

Whether you are an organization, university or individual, we work with a variety of clients for speaking engagements, trainings and digital storytelling services, including social media strategy, photography and videography. For any inquires, please email Kevin at kevin@thenichemovement.com.

Press:

If you would like to be featured in one of our upcoming interviews or you would like to interview The Niche Movement team, please email Lara at lara@thenichemovement.com.

I Love my Job:

We are continuing to feature people that love what they do. If you or someone you know loves their job and has found their niche, email Robyn at robyn@thenichemovement.com for an interview.

Bulk Book Orders:

If you would like to order bulk book orders for your business or organization, please contact Kevin at kevin@thenichemovement.com.

Thank you for reading.

- Kevin

Notes

[i] "The Enormous Cost of Unhappy Employees." Inc.com. Web. 16 June

[ii] Berger, Warren. "Find Your Passion With These 8 Thought-Provoking Questions." Co.Design. 14 Apr. 2014. Web. 16 June 2015. <http://www.fastcodesign.com/3028946/find-your-passion-with-these-8-thought-provoking-questions>.

[iii] O'Boyle, Ed, and Jim Harter. "Report: State of the Global Workplace." *Report: State of the Global Workplace.* Gallup, Inc., 22 Sept. 2014. Web. 16 June 2015. <http://www.gallup.com/services/176735/state-global-workplace.aspx>.

[iv] "What Is Bias?" *Psychology Today.* Sussex Publishers, LLC. Web. 16 June 2015. <https://www.psychologytoday.com/basics/bias>.

[v] O'Boyle, Ed, and Jim Harter. "Report: State of the Global Workplace." *Report: State of the Global Workplace.* Gallup, Inc., 22 Sept. 2014. Web. 16 June 2015. <http://www.gallup.com/services/176735/state-global-workplace.aspx>.

[vi] Jones, Benjamin, E.J. Reedy, and Bruce A. Weinberg. "AGE AND SCIENTIFIC GENIUS." *National Bureau of Economic Research.* National Bureau of Economic Research, 2014. Web. 16 June 2015. <http://www.nber.org/papers/w19866.pdf>.

[vii] Alhanati, Joao. "Follow Your Passions And Success Will Follow." *Investopedia.* Investopedia, LLC., 9 July 2013. Web. 16 June 2015. <http://www.investopedia.com/articles/pf/12/passion-success.asp>.

[viii] Green, Alison. "Why You Shouldn't Follow Your Passion." *US News & World Report - Money.* U.S. News & World Report LP., 17 Apr. 2013. Web. 16 June 2015. <http://money.usnews.com/money/blogs/outside-voices-careers/2013/04/17/why-you-shouldnt-follow-your-passion>.

[ix] Tucker, Kenneth A. "A Passion for Work." *Gallup - Business Journal.* Gallup, Inc., 18 Feb. 2002. Web. 16 June 2015. <http://www.gallup.com/businessjournal/379/passion-work.aspx>.

[x] Henry, Alan. "The Science of Breaking Out of Your Comfort Zone (and Why You Should)." *Lifehacker.* The Gawker Media Group, 3 July 2013. Web. 16 June 2015. <http://lifehacker.com/the-science-of-breaking-out-of-your-comfort-zone-and-w-656426705>.

[xi] Cabane, Olivia Fox. *The Charisma Myth: How Anyone Can Master the Art and Science of Personal Magnetism*. New York: Penguin Group (USA), 2012. Print.

[xii] Szalavitz, Maia. "Q&A: Q&A with Susan Cain on the Power of Introverts." *Time*. Time Inc., 27 Jan. 2012. Web. 16 June 2015. <http://healthland.time.com/2012/01/27/mind-reading-qa-with-susan-cain-on-the-power-of-introverts/>.

[xiii] Hixon, Todd. "Higher Education Is Now Ground Zero For Disruption." *Forbes*. Forbes.com LLC™, 6 Jan. 2014. Web. 16 June 2015. <http://www.forbes.com/sites/toddhixon/2014/01/06/higher-education-is-now-ground-zero-for-disruption/>.

[xiv] Chan, Andy, and Tommy Derry. "A Roadmap for Transforming the College-To-Career Experience." *Rethinking Success*. Wake Forest University, 1 May 2013. Web. 16 June 2015. <http://rethinkingsuccess.wfu.edu/files/2013/05/A-Roadmap-for-Transforming-The-College-to-Career-Experience.pdf>.

[xv] Chan, Andy, and Tommy Derry. "A Roadmap for Transforming the College-To-Career Experience." *Rethinking Success*. Wake Forest University, 1 May 2013. Web. 16 June 2015. <http://rethinkingsuccess.wfu.edu/files/2013/05/A-Roadmap-for-Transforming-The-College-to-Career-Experience.pdf>.

[xvi] Koo, Youngeun, and Paul Kilty. "In Search of Employment: An Insight into How Young People Look for Work." *Wereprezent*. Reprezent, 20 Mar. 2014. Web. 16 June 2015. <http://media.wereprezent.s3.amazonaws.com/news/wp-content/uploads/2014/03/Reprezent_In-search-of-employment_Full-report_March-2014.pdf>.

[xvii] Marte, Jonnelle. "Is Graduate School worth the Cost? Here's How to Know." *Washington Post*. The WP Company LLC, 2 Dec. 2014. Web. 16 June 2015. <http://www.washingtonpost.com/news/get-there/wp/2014/12/02/is-graduate-school-worth-the-cost-heres-how-to-know/>.

[xviii] Heffernan, Virginia. "Education Needs a Digital-Age Upgrade." *Opinionator*. The New York Times Company, 7 Aug. 2011. Web. 16 June 2015. <http://opinionator.blogs.nytimes.com/2011/08/07/education-needs-a-digital-age-upgrade/?_r=0>.

[xix] Swallow, Erica. "A Field Guide to Solo Entrepreneurship." *The Huffington Post*. TheHuffingtonPost.com, Inc., 7 May 2013. Web. 16

June 2015. <http://www.huffingtonpost.com/erica-swallow/a-field-guide-to-solo-ent_b_3211321.html>.

[xx] "Engagement Study: Summer Is a Good Time to Win the Hearts and Minds of Employees." *Randstad*. Randstad USA, 17 June 2013. Web. 16 June 2015. <https://www.randstadusa.com/workforce360/employer-branding/summertime-employee-engagement/102/>.

[xxi] O'Boyle, Ed, and Jim Harter. "Report: State of the Global Workplace." *Report: State of the Global Workplace*. Gallup, Inc., 22 Sept. 2014. Web. 16 June 2015. <http://www.gallup.com/services/176735/state-global-workplace.aspx>.

[xxii] O'Connell, Courtney. "7 (little Known) Digital Reputation Stats and How to Use Them to Your Advantage." *Socialnomics*. Socialnomics, 25 July 2014. Web. 16 June 2015. <http://www.socialnomics.net/2014/07/25/7-little-known-digital-reputation-stats-and-how-to-use-them-to-your-advantage/>.

[xxiii] Kasper, Kimberley. "2014 Jobvite Job Seeker Nation Study." *Jobvite*. Jobvite, Inc., 19 Mar. 2014. Web. 16 June 2015. <http://web.jobvite.com/rs/jobvite/images/2014 Job Seeker Survey.pdf>.

[xxiv] "Millennials at Work: Reshaping the Workplace." *Millennials Survey*. PwC, 2011. Web. 16 June 2015. <http://www.pwc.com/gx/en/managing-tomorrows-people/future-of-work/assets/reshaping-the-workplace.pdf>.

[xxv] Zanella, Silvia, and Ivana Pais. "#SocialRecruiting: A Global Study." *Adecco*. Adecco, 2 June 2014. Web. 16 June 2015. <http://www.adecco.com/en-US/Industry-Insights/Documents/social-recruiting/adecco-global-social-recruiting-survey-global-report.pdf>.

[xxvi] Kasper, Kimberley. "2014 Jobvite Job Seeker Nation Study." *Jobvite*. Jobvite, Inc., 19 Mar. 2014. Web. 16 June 2015. <http://web.jobvite.com/rs/jobvite/images/2014 Job Seeker Survey.pdf>.

[xxvii] Di Meglio, Francesca. "College Startups: The 'New Master's Degree'" *Bloomberg Business Week*. Bloomberg, 26 Mar. 2013. Web. 16 June 2015. <http://www.businessweek.com/articles/2013-03-26/college-startups-the-new-masters-degree>.

[xxviii] Jones, Holly. "'Treat Your Career like a Bad Boyfriend': Life Tips from Amy Poehler's Book." *Womens Agenda*. Private Media Pty Ltd., 7 Nov. 2014. Web. 16 June 2015. <http://www.womensagenda.com.au/talking-about/top-stories/treat-

your-career-like-a-bad-boyfriend-life-tips-from-amy-poehler-s-book/201411074870#.VVoI0pNViko>.

[xxix] Saisan, Joanna, Melinda Smith, and Gina Kemp. "Volunteering and Its Surprising Benefits." *HelpGuide*. Helpguide.org, 1 Apr. 2015. Web. 16 June 2015. <http://www.helpguide.org/articles/work-career/volunteering-and-its-surprising-benefits.htm>.

[xxx] Schulte, Brigid. "Millennials Want a Work-life Balance. Their Bosses Just Don't Get Why." *Washington Post*. The Washington Post, 5 May 2015. Web. 16 June 2015. <http://www.washingtonpost.com/local/millennials-want-a-work-life-balance-their-bosses-just-dont-get-why/2015/05/05/1859369e-f376-11e4-84a6-6d7c67c50db0_story.html?wprss=rss_AllWPStoriesandBlogs&tid=sm_fb>.

[xxxi] Ridge, S. Brent. "Balance: The New Workplace Perk." *Forbes*. Forbes.com LLC™ , 19 Mar. 2007. Web. 16 June 2015. <http://www.forbes.com/2007/03/19/work-life-health-lead-careers-worklife07-cz_sr_0319ridge.html>.

[xxxii] Ridge, S. Brent. "Balance: The New Workplace Perk." *Forbes*. Forbes.com LLC™ , 19 Mar. 2007. Web. 16 June 2015. <http://www.forbes.com/2007/03/19/work-life-health-lead-careers-worklife07-cz_sr_0319ridge.html>.

[xxxiii] Kaling, Mindy. *Is Everyone Hanging Out Without Me? (And Other Concerns)*. New York: Crown Archetype, 2011. Print.

[xxxiv] Nishi, Dennis. "Take Your Search for a Job Offline." *The Wall Street Journal*. Dow Jones & Company, Inc., 24 Mar. 2013. Web. 16 June 2015. <http://online.wsj.com/article/SB10001424127887323869604578368733437346820.html?mod=e2fb>.

[xxxv] Davies, Simon. "Career Change Statistics: How Many Times Will You Change Jobs in Your Life?" *Careers Advice Online*. Careers Advice Online. Web. 16 June 2015. <http://www.careers-advice-online.com/career-change-statistics.html>.

[xxxvi] Sandberg, Sheryl, and Nell Scovell. *Lean In*. Print.